THE
FORTY
PLUS
HANDBOOK

THE FORTY PLUS HANDBOOK

The Fine Art of
Growing Older

DAVID RAY

Printed in the United States of America
ISBN 0-8499-2850-8
Library of Congress Catalog Card Number: 78-65799

First Printing, April 1979
Second Printing, July 1979

Contents

A Word to the Reader

Aging is the most significant and dramatic phenomenon of our day. In industrialized nations, people are living longer and the birthrate is declining. As a result, a shift in the social structure is underway.

Government, industry, and the Church must adopt more adequate approaches to deal with older persons. In new ways, the younger generation must face the power and presence of the older crowd. Middle-agers and older persons themselves must develop a winsome approach to getting older, a kind which spotlights the *whole* person—needs, realities, abilities, opportunities, and vast potential.

The reasons for this book are simple:

1. *Information:* To outline seven major needs faced by middle-aged people and nine major needs in retirement living and to make some suggestions by which to meet those needs.
2. *Inspiration:* To motivate people of influence in government, business, and the Church; to encourage individuals of all ages—most assuredly you, the readers—to do something positive about the needs.
3. *Application:* To urge acceptance and application of the principles, programs, and steps pointed out in this book, including wholesome attitudes and spiritual wholeness for living *and* dying.

To be more specific, I pray this book will serve the following purposes:

1. Encourage a deeper and more successful concept of *growing* older.
2. Emphasize action "with, by, and for" retired persons instead of maintaining the old, worn-out, debilitating

syndrome of helplessness which government, society, industry, and the Church have inflicted on older people, and to which many older persons have resigned themselves.

3. Energize middle-aged people to start planning for retirement twenty years in advance of actual retirement. Yes, beginning when you are forty years of age!

4. Erase some absurd myths which surround the aging process and which have given birth to deep-rooted fear of aging.

5. Eradicate flimsy ideas about the capabilities and worthwhileness of the forty-plus generation.

Henri Frederic Amiel, the nineteenth-century Swiss philosopher, said, "To know how to grow old is the masterwork of wisdom, and one of the most difficult chapters in the great art of living." [1] My hope is that you will gain new knowledge and insight to grow older and act upon what you read. "A truly good book," according to Henry Thoreau, "teaches me better than to read it. I must soon lay it down and commence living on its hint. . . . What I began by reading I must finish by acting." [2]

This is my fifth book, but I have never felt more strongly about the need for the message conveyed in a book than I do about this one. Maybe it's because of a great assurance: "The godly shall flourish. . . . Even in old age they will still produce fruit and be vital and green" (Ps. 92:12, 14, LB). Let's believe it! Let's live it!

Growing older and enjoying it!
DAVID RAY

1.

On Your Mark . . . Get Set For Retirement

*"Growing old gracefully should
begin with youth."*
—*Walter Beran Wolfe*

If you are over forty, you are part of one of the largest population explosions in the present century. Perhaps you haven't realized that the percentage of the population in the United States which is over age forty-five is growing at twice the rate of those under forty-five. Over twenty-five percent of the population is past sixty. If current trends continue, in twenty years this segment will increase to thirty-three percent, and one-half of the population will be at least fifty.

Possibly you haven't realized that about one person out of five in the Western world is retired, that now, in the United States, retirees make up over eleven percent of the population. In twenty-five years, the number of people over sixty-five has grown from twelve million to some twenty-five million. And more than eight million Americans are over seventy-five.

It is an older-person phenomenon which is rivaling the baby boom of the 1940s and the youth culture of the 1950s and 60s. And the trend in America is largely that of other industrialized nations.

On the average, people retiring these days can look forward to another fifteen years of life. Researchers are discovering cures for strokes, heart disease, blindness, and deterioration of the central nervous system. Scientists at a number of centers, including Duke University, the Univer-

9

sity of Michigan, and the University of California, are trying to discover how and why cells are born, age, and die. The breakthroughs these scientists are enjoying are increasing longevity at a phenomenal rate.

Dr. Richard Davis, researcher at the Ethel Percy Andrus Gerontology Center at the University of Southern California, says that the time may be upon us when it will be normal to live to be one hundred years old. "We're not talking about a miracle pill or a magic wand. Science is now . . . to the point where the average life span can be increased by *many* years." And Dr. Bernard Strehler, professor of biology at the University of Southern California, writes, "The postponement of physical and mental senescence will mean that a person of sixty will have the outlook of a person of fifty; a person of seventy, the outlook of a person of fifty-six; and a person of ninety, the outlook of a person of seventy." [1]

The increase in longevity means that, by the time some of us retire, we may have an average of twenty more years to look forward to. Think of it—half as many years as an entire lifespan a few generations ago! Beyond a doubt, retirement is an enormous step in a person's life. It is one which yells for diligent and thoughtful planning. The purpose of this chapter is to suggest ways men and women in their middle years can prepare for those important retirement years.

But first, let's define retirement. *Retirement is the termination from the vocation upon which you depend for livelihood.* This can happen at various ages but in our country it usually occurs around age sixty-five.

Let's define middle age. A few years ago, the American Medical Association sponsored a Quality of Life Conference in Chicago. The consensus of the meeting was that middle age actually begins around age twenty-five! Of course, such news rattled a younger generation. The Conference went on to list three segments of middle age—beginning middle age (25–34), middle middle age (35–54), and maturing middle age (55–64).[2] However, *for my purposes, I identify middle age as forty to retirement.* These make up the bulk of a person's employment years.

My experiences with and observations of middle-aged persons have led me to believe there are seven major needs most people face during these years, needs which encompass the four areas of the person's makeup—physical, emotional, social, and spiritual. They are:

1) *Development as a complete person.* You must become more than what you do to put a roof over your head and food on your table!

2) *Discovery of deeper meaning.* Your life and job yearn for this meaning.

3) *Enjoyable and growing relationships.* They are important to your spouse, others, and—most assuredly—you!

4) *Positive attitude.* This is an environment of mind by which to make middle age happy and rewarding, and to meet the demands of everyday life with an inner plus.

5) *A wholesome concept of growing older.* This replaces that dilapidated, defeating, and taboo-saturated idea that aging is a curse! It repels the silly bombardment of helplessness thrown at you as you grow older.

6) *Spiritual vitality.* A widening and deepening faith in Jesus Christ opens to you new vistas of living!

7) *Thoughtful planning for retirement.* You need to experience retirement on the installment plan instead of a last-minute crash program. Middle age, even twenty years in advance of retirement, is the time to start. This chapter and the next will outline ten rules for retirement preparation which you can put to use in your middle years.

TEN RULES FOR
RETIREMENT PREPARATION

1. Begin Planning Your Retirement . . . Now!

In my opinion, planning needs to begin twenty years before retirement. "Twenty years!" a man exclaimed in my seminar. "Why, I'm only forty-three. I'm not even at the top of my 'productive' years yet! And you say I should start getting ready for retirement now?"

My answer: A resounding YES!

The reason is quite elementary. There is a certain continuity to your entire life—a continuity which moves with you from one stage of life into the next. What you are in the middle years commonly is heightened in older years; for instance, a grouchy, selfish, tyrannical, possessive, difficult, loud-mouthed personality at fifty will normally be a grouchy, selfish, tyrannical, possessive, difficult, loud-mouthed personality at seventy! A loving, benevolent, happy-thinking, fair-minded, outgoing personality at forty-eight will normally be a loving, benevolent, happy-thinking, fair-minded, outgoing personality at sixty-eight!

Those who let retirement catch them off-guard are more apt to be bored and feel hurt in the leisure years. They are defeated by older years unless they do a lot of catching up! Instead of a reliable and decent transition, they are stunned by the sudden fact of retirement. As one woman told me, "Retirement is like jumping into icy water."

At age thirty-four, my wife and I started planning for retirement. I believe it was one of the wisest, most God-guided decisions we have ever made. *The retirement years are best accomplished on the installment plan!* The plan is by stages, not a fairy-tale, pie-in-the-sky, crash method. The time to start is while you are in your forties or, at the latest, in your early fifties. Industry would better fulfil the moral, emotional, and social obligation it has to employees by providing seminars on retirement planning for employees and making attendance mandatory for workers who are forty-five years of age and older!

Dr. Matthew E. Fairbanks, assistant professor of medicine and community health at the University of Rochester, New York, says, "Old age should be a period of fulfillment, freedom, and, indeed accomplishment. . . . Retirement is a whole new career, a whole new way of life for which everyone should make preparations." With remarkable insight, Dr. Fairbanks continues, "Retirement means planning ahead for health, economic satisfaction, and happiness for you and your partner." [3]

2. Make Your Life Meaningful

I mentioned a few pages ago the Quality of Life Congress sponsored by the American Medical Association to deal with problems of middle age.

Dr. Wallace Anne Wesley, who directed the Congress, cited problems in the middle years as drug dependency, divorce, child-rearing, and sexual adjustment. She said, "The really big problem . . . is one of a sense of identity." Interpreted, I see these questions: "Who am I, really? What's the basic meaning of *my* life?"

Dr. Viktor E. Frankl, the European psychiatrist, maintains that a person's primary need is to find a sense of meaning for his life. He states, "Man's main concern is not to gain pleasure or to avoid pain, but rather to see a meaning in his life."[4] If meaning is there, he can truly enjoy pleasure and endure pain with a measure of success.

But the sense of meaning is often clouded. H. E. Martz tells about a successful business executive who retired from his job, sold his luxurious city condominium, and moved to the woods of Maine where he took up pottery making. When writing to a friend, he explained, "The trouble with modern life is that the urgent things crowd out the *important* ones." Andrew Sarris expounds on the problem further when he says, " 'Making it,' to most of us, means making a living, making a killing, and making a life. Unfortunately, we make it only to the first or second rung on the ladder. We're so preoccupied with making a living and making a killing that we don't get around to making a life."[5]

The Rockefeller Report on Education adds, "What most people want—young or old—is not more security, or comfort, or luxury, although they are glad enough to have these. Most of all, they want *meaning* in their lives. If our era and our culture and our leaders do not, or cannot, offer great meanings, great objectives, great convictions, then people will settle for shallow and trivial substitutes. People who live aimlessly, who are satisfied by shoddy experiences, have simply not been stirred by alternative meanings—religious meanings, ethical values, ideals of social and civic responsibility, or high standards of self-fulfillment." [6]

Professor Lucius Bugbee shares an experience which speaks for middle-agers, too. One morning, a graduate student in one of the science departments at the university phoned him and asked if he might come over to see Dr. Bugbee immediately. In a few minutes, the student burst into the Professor's office and, without any word of introduction, said with unusual emotion, "Can you tell me what it is all about, this business of living? What are we here for?" He admonished, "Don't give me any more facts. I am fed up on fact. I want meanings and values!" [7]

If your life now is void of meaning, your later years will also be void of meaning unless you undergo significant changes between today and retirement! Remember, there is a continuity to your whole life. I once read a story which reminds me of this.

The scene is Paris. A young man follows another person, wanting to know whether this other person rooms at a certain hotel. To get this information without arousing the suspicion of the hotel clerk, the hero decides to try a trick. He asks the clerk whether his own name is on the register, planning to look down the list as the clerk scans the register, and thereby discover the name and room number of the other man.

To the hero's amazement, the clerk looks up and says, "Yes, he is here and he's been waiting for you. He's in Room 40. I will have you shown right up." There is nothing the hero can do except go through with his plan, so he follows the bellhop. He walks into Room 40 and finds a man remarkably like himself, only slightly grey around the hairline and a bit heavier. It is himself as he will be at age forty, twenty years away. [8]

If you were to meet yourself at age sixty-five, what would you see? It depends on the meaning—deep meaning—to life you possess today, or the meaning you develop from this time on. A clear contrast is reflected in the following two verses. At age thirty-six, Lord Byron wrote:

My days are in the yellow leaf;
   The flowers and fruits of love are gone;
The worm, the canker, and the grief,
   Are mine alone! [9]

Robert Browning showed meaning and excitement when he penned:

Grow old along with me!
The best is yet to be,
The last of life, for which the first was made:
  Our times are in His hand
  Who saith 'A whole I planned,
Youth shows but half; trust God: see all nor be afraid! [10]

Here are some ways to discover great meaning in life:

1) *Think of your life as more than things.* Dr. Darrold Treffert claims that the modern feeling that life is meaningless is in part a result of the "American fairy tale." We have been led to believe that success means having two cars, a swimming pool, a wife or husband, and beautiful children. These are not to be undermined, but more basic is developing warm human relationships, honesty in expressing yourself, a sense of order and hope for the future, a sense that you belong to something larger than yourself which is worthwhile, and a maturing into life made through your own efforts.[11]

2) *Become a steamboat in life instead of a sailboat.* Occasionally, I have watched sailboats. They are at the mercy of wind and waves. To be sure, there is a need to take advantage of wind and waves in life, but to listlessly, thoughtlessly be pushed around by circumstances and conditions? A steamboat can use wind and waves and move regardless of them. There is power inside.

3) *Turn hurricanes into helpmates.* There are three approaches to adversity. One is the *whiner* who complains, "Oh, me! Why me!" Another is the *diner* who attempts to cover it in superficial answers which don't actually answer anything. Then, there is the *miner* who digs at the possibilities in an

adversity and turns it into some sort of advantage. Emily Dickinson described the miner:

> Fate slew him, but he did not drop;
> She felled—he did not fall—
> Impaled him on her fiercest stakes—
> He neutralized them all.[12]

4) *Have some quiet time each day.* This is time when you, on the level of human consciousness, reach in and out to your God, the source of bona-fide meaning. Dr. Frank Laubach was a genuine Christian meditator. As a result of meditation, he says, "I think more clearly. I forget less frequently. Things which I did with a strain before I now do easily. . . . I worry about nothing, and lose no sleep. . . . Even the mirror reveals a new light in my eyes and face. I no longer feel in a hurry about anything. Each minute I meet calmly. . . . Nothing can go wrong excepting one thing. That is, that God may slip from my mind if I do not keep on my guard. If He is there, the universe is with me. My task is simple and clear." [13]

Hannah of the Old Testament gets to the heart of the matter: "My heart thrills to the Eternal, my powers are heightened by my God" (1 Sam. 2:1, Moffatt).

3. Accept the Process of Getting Older

The next step in getting ready for retirement is this: Accept the process of growing older. A man who came to my office expressed the honest feelings of people who dread advancing age. "I'm over the fear of dying. I'm afraid to live!"

This fact is inevitable: You're older now than when you began to read this book. Of course, there is an alternative—a six-foot-deep burial plot in the cemetery. Considering that alternative, getting older looks pretty good!

The process involves changes. It was only in fun that loveable George Burns, the American comedian, said as he celebrated his birthday, "I'm doing at eighty what I did at eighteen, which goes to show what a dull boy I was when I was eighteen."

Accept the process like the sixty-ish woman who gave me a copy of "My Get Up And Go Has Got Up And Went":

> How do I know that my youth is all spent?
> Well, my get up and go has got up and went.
> But in spite of it all, I am able to grin
> When I think of the places my get up has been.
>
> Old age is golden, so I've heard it said,
> But sometimes I wonder as I get into bed,
> With my ears in a drawer, my teeth in a cup,
> My eyes on the table until I wake up.
>
> Ere sleep dims my eyes, I say to myself,
> Is there anything else I should lay on the shelf?
> And I am happy to say as I close my door,
> My friends are the same, only perhaps even more.
>
> When I was young, my slippers were red,
> I could kick up my heels right over my head.
> When I grew older my slippers were blue,
> But still I could dance the whole night through.
>
> Now I am old, my slippers are black,
> I walk to the store and puff my way back.
> The reason I know my youth is all spent.
> My get up and go has got up and went.
>
> But I don't really mind, when I think with a grin
> Of all the grand places my get up has been.
> Since I retired from life's competition,
> I busy myself with complete repetition.
>
> I get up each morning, dust off my wits,
> Pick up the paper and read the obits.
> If my name is missing, I know I'm not dead,
> So, I eat a good breakfast and go back to bed.

On the other hand, if you fight the aging process, you freeze up spiritually, emotionally, socially, and even physically. You begin to withdraw into a shell. Physical capacities begin to diminish. Growing older demands some of the following changes:

1) *Age dictates that you work smarter rather than harder.* Get more results from less time spent on the job by planning your work, then working your plan.

2) *Set priorities for your workday.* What are the essential jobs you need to do? What must be done today?

3) *Efficiently use your time.* Make the most out of the higher energy periods. For many, earlier in the day is peak energy time.

4) *Put your experience and knowledge to maximum use.* In youth, you probably valued enthusiasm over experience. I remember when I was asked, in 1970, to put in booklet form some information for parents which I had used in a series of family-life talks. Confidently and boldly, I proceeded to assemble the materials, feeling a sense of pride that someone would actually think they were worthwhile to print. I entitled the booklet "Ten Commandments for Moms and Dads," and it mainly dealt with relationships to teenage children. Afterwards, my children became teenagers. I began to think that a better title would be "Ten Suggestions for Moms and Dads." After that, my children became more teen-agy teenagers. Now, I feel that the title should be changed to "Ten Possible Hints, Maybe, For Moms and Dads."

Now, you have experience and knowledge. These are precious, irreplaceable, very valuable assets. This is the time for you to integrate them into a more powerful team for your good. But don't let them turn off the brain!

4. Think Ahead Financially

By the time a person gets into his forties or fifties, he is usually through the higher expense years which the requirements of life made necessary. The children are grown and on their own—at least, they should be! Mortgage payments are reduced and income is higher.

There is no need to be a scrooge. At the same time, your

monthly budget must include savings and/or investments which can be used for living expenses during retirement years. Besides, regular saving is good discipline for an altogether too undisciplined society.

The amount put in an interest-bearing account or investment (with reliable promise of fair growth!) is not the primary issue. Instead, it is a plan and a program on which you begin, then persist. For example, fifty dollars a month in a regular savings account for twenty years will amount to over nineteen thousand dollars when an interest yield of five percent is compounded annually. One hundred dollars a month for twenty years will exceed thirty-eight thousand dollars. And this is using a very conservative percentage yield. Due to present circumstances, saving by steps may be necessary. For instance, begin at a lower figure and, over the years, increase the amount. How do you put it together?

Reasonably project the monthly income you will need in retirement years. Be sure to include the inflationary factor, possibly eight to ten percent a year. Tabulate other sources of retirement income such as Social Security, pension plan, cash from life insurance, etc. (An insurance man and Social Security representative can be of help.) Total the other sources of income and subtract that figure from your projected need, then adopt a program of savings and/or investments that will get you as close to your retirement income figure as possible. In this way, you might avoid the "half as much money" syndrome under which some retirees now suffer.

Whether the amount you put in savings and/or investments at the outset is ten dollars or a thousand dollars a month, agree on a plan and get going. But allow enough to enjoy life along the way and to support your church and other worthy causes.

Another decision my wife and I made when I was thirty-four years of age was that, as much as possible, we would do before retirement what we should like to do after we retire, if we had the money. To us, this has become an enjoyment of life along the way. After all, neither of us has the guarantee that both or either will live to retirement! Neither do you!

What we have done has not interrupted our overall financial plans for retirement. It has been a matter of priorities. Example: a big, luxurious, gas-guzzling car and no trip, or a more economical car and trip? The most expensive room in the hotel, or an adequate room? By management of what income we do have, we have been able to travel, yet rear a family, pay the bills, and begin plans for retirement.

5. Start Now to Grow the Habit of Showing Happiness

There are two immutable laws which I emphasize in seminars. They are:

> *The Law of Highest Attention:* Whatever captures your utmost attention will replace the results of lower attention.

> *The Law of Deepest Desire and Expectation:* What you desire and expect the most supplants lesser wants and desires.

What you consistently give your thoughts to and what you intensely want and expect comes to pass.

Author George Shinn talks about a man who married a beautiful girl and moved into a beautiful neighborhood after their honeymoon. After the lights were flipped off that first night, she nudged her husband and said, "Jim, there's a burglar downstairs." Jim replied, "Honey, there's no burglar downstairs, but if you insist I'll go check it out." The next night, the same thing: "There's a burglar downstairs." And the next, and next, and next, and next! This went on for seventeen years. Every night, he trekked downstairs looking for the burglar. Over the years, it even began to threaten their marriage.

One night, she tugged at Jim again: "Sweetheart, no doubt about it, there's a burglar downstairs this time." "Now, listen," Sweetheart insisted, "I've hunted this burglar for seventeen years. He hasn't shown up yet, so I'm not going down again!" She pleaded, "Please, for me! I can't sleep! He's there! I know it! Just go and see for yourself!" Jim draped his robe around him for the umpteenth time and made the all-too-familiar journey downstairs. This time there was a burglar! He had a gun in his hand and he was pillaging the den.

Jim said, "Friend, go right on with what you're doing. Get anything your heart desires. I won't call the police if you will do me one favor. When you get through here, come upstairs with me. I want you to meet my wife because she has been looking for you for seventeen years!" [14]

If you are serious about an enjoyable retirement, start growing the habit of showing happiness. It will produce a strength even when there are unhappy happenings. Your personality will develop on the brighter side of life. Life takes on a more significant meaning because things will not be allowed to keep you down. The way to start developing the habit of showing happiness is not really difficult and you can begin today:

1) *Search out the good in everybody and everything.*

2) *Look on the brightest side.*

3) *Anticipate the best.*

Thomas Carlyle, the outstanding Scottish essayist in the eighteen hundreds, wrote, "Our grand business in life is not to see what lies dimly at a distance, but to do what lies clearly at hand." [15] This is a challenging summation for this chapter. What lies clearly at hand for you is, "On Your Mark . . . Get Ready . . . For Retirement." Let's continue our "Ten Rules for Retirement Preparation" in the next chapter.

2.

Retirement: Boom or Bust?

"One of the many things nobody ever tells you about middle age is that it's such a nice change from being young."
—Dorothy Canfield

We have already pointed out that retirement life is so important that up to twenty years should be invested in preparing for it. A retired couple said, "Mr. Ray, if we only knew at forty-six what we have learned at sixty-six in this seminar!" In this chapter, we continue with the Ten Rules for Retirement Preparation:

6. Step by Step, Change from Making a Living to Making a Life

Your work provides a contrast to leisure and the opportunity to express yourself through creative endeavor. Leisure offers a contrast to work—a re-creation, a slacking-off, a different direction. In the employment years, all work and no play makes a very dull day, not to mention a very stale life!

The central theme in step-by-step change from making a living to making a life is this: *First, you are a person; second, you are a worker!* The person is more than a machine, more than a production line, and more than a producer. You are more than what you do for a living. Here we meet head-on the classic work ethic.

From 1870 to 1975, the average workweek in the United States went from about 66 hours to 38.7 hours. Yet, from

23

our beginnings, we have been trained for labor to the extent that production has become a god. Our value as persons has been measured by our ability to put out, to perform. In the meanwhile, *being* has been relegated to second, or third, or fourth seat behind *doing*. Instead of the person giving dignity and significance to work, work has given dignity and significance to the person.

Now, you must reverse this order in your life. Otherwise, when you no longer choose to be employed or you are forced by circumstances or age to retire, you will suffer a total loss of your value as a person.

Business need not be alarmed that this approach will create a mass of moochers, a society of loafers, and a reduction in production. To the contrary, the most valuable employee is the one who has an honest appreciation for *who* he is—a person—in contrast to *what* he does—work. *What* you do is drastically affected by *who* you are, as you see yourself. *You are a who, not a what!*

The person who holds himself in value is the one of greatest value to the company! One who is important in selected areas of interest, in addition to his role as a producer, frees himself mentally, physically, and emotionally to become a more important producer! Therefore, get a grip on yourself as a person and diversify your interests. Here's how:

1) *Take a hard look at your life now to determine where you are and what you need to do.* Are you in control or are you controlled? Are you a victim or a victor?

2) *Organize your interests.* Pinpoint them so as not to spread yourself too thin. Examples: golf, fishing, gardening, games, do-it-yourself projects, hobbies, travel, church and civic programs.

3) *Make yourself as useful as you can.* You can find new ways to offer your services and new services to offer—a new and improved way of doing an old thing.

4) *Do your best while you're at work, then leave the work at work.* There is a satisfying sense of well-being when you realize you have done the job to the best of your ability. The process of re-creation for the next day of productive work re-

quires that you finish your work for the day. Let it lie and resume the next day refreshed and revitalized.

Some people have developed a second career by diversifying their interests. G. H. Harris, a friend of mine in Jackson, Mississippi, has been an avid fisherman for years. While in his fifties and the real estate business, he began tinkering with the idea of a silent motor which would make it possible to move the boat without disturbing the fish in the water below. At his leisure, over a ten-year period, G. H. worked on the idea in his garage. It resulted in the Motor Guide which now has been bought by thousands of fishermen.

7. Shape Up

Make the effort necessary to keep your body in shape. All too often, middle age is the flabby, paunchy, roly-poly age. I, for one, can appreciate what a fifty-year-old friend meant when he said, "I hate going to the beach. Have you ever tried to hold your stomach in for six hours?" The little exercise many tend to do was described by Jackie Gleason: "When I wake up each morning, I always say sternly to myself: 'Ready, now. Up. Down. Up. Down. Up. Down.' After three strenuous minutes, I tell myself, 'Okay, boy, now we'll try the other eyelid.' "

A prominent physician explained to me the two changes which can occur between youth and middle age. They are metabolism and activity. The chemical composition of the body may alter, but more importantly, the activity level reduces while the eating level continues unabated. There is more sitting and TV watching, less physical exertion, but calorie intake remains as high as in the teen years. Consequently, the devastating, all-too-apparent middle-age bulge and multiple chins.

I am six feet, six inches tall, and I once weighed one hundred ninety pounds. Yet I ate like my stomach was a bottomless pit. I could consume twelve tacos in one meal and a gallon of cold, refreshing, sweet milk a day without batting an eye. Then came age twenty-five when the very sight of milk created another belt of fat around the mid-section. Now I languish with skim milk which my wife teasingly refers to as "grey water." Since age twenty-five, I have probably gained and lost at least three hundred pounds all total! Not long ago, I went for my annual physical examination. As the doctor watched me get on the scales, I said, "There's not much telling what we'll see." He looked at the reading and said, "I'll not tell what we just saw!" Promptly, he handed me a twelve-hundred-calorie-a-day diet!

Arnold H. Glasgow reminds us that our body is the baggage we carry through life—the more excess baggage, the shorter the trip.[1] An old Irish recipe for longevity reads, "Leave the table hungry, the bed sleepy, and the tavern thirsty." St. Paul wrote, "Your body is a temple of the Holy Spirit" (1 Corinthians 6:19, RSV). Webster's dictionary defines "temple" as a locality or place appropriate for the dwelling of God. Even the prophet Isaiah, thousands of years before Paul, referred to the relationship of the body to mind and spirit. "Why will you earn fresh strokes, for holding on in your revolt? Your whole head is sick, your whole heart is diseased; from the sole of the foot to the head, no part is sound" (1:5–6, Moffatt). Here are some pointers for keeping your body in shape:

1) *Avoid slouchy habits.* In jest, Franklin P. Jones claimed that everybody should have a few bad habits so his friends won't suspect him of something worse. If you allow room, you will stumble into habits that really inhibit life: Too much television, too little reading, reading materials that blast life instead of building it, and unhealthy language. A good bit of advice was given to me one time. *Never start anything you can't stop!* There is one unerring way to stop a habit that needs to be stopped and that is to stop doing it. It may be like getting up an ascending staircase one step at a time, but it's a beginning.

2) *Have complete physical checkups regularly, at least once a year.* It is one of the wisest investments you can make!

3) *Watch the kinds of foods you eat.* A healthful menu

has healing power in it, but the horrendous combinations we enjoy! My children think the super meal includes both macaroni and mashed potatoes! Get more protein and calcium and fewer fats and carbohydrates.

4) *Watch the amount of food you eat.* Overeating is the almost irrepressible problem! For most people, the best weight for middle and retirement years is the same they were at age twenty-five. Unfortunately, it requires thirty percent fewer calories!

5) *Exercise properly and regularly.* This means *each day!* On a vacation, it did my heart good to see a woman well into her seventies participate in the morning exercise group. "Unwrinkles my bones," she said. And to see another lady, in her eighties and crippled, getting around, sunning, moving about, and talking to us. Curling up and withering was not for her! You may not be a Monty Montgomery, age sixty-five, who ran a twenty-six mile marathon in two hours, thirty minutes. You may not be a Herbert Schmidt, who high-jumped twelve feet, nine and one-half inches at age sixty-one. Or Dr. Paul Spangler, who at seventy-seven ran six miles in forty-seven minutes and fifty-one seconds! But you are you, and your body is capable of much more than you probably give it credit for.

Check with your doctor to make sure more strenuous exercises are okay. I walk about two miles each day, but it is a fast walk. I have long legs! Some people have to jog to keep up. You can exercise ten to fifteen minutes at home or in your office. Perhaps you have access to a YMCA. Swimming is a comprehensive exercise. So is tennis. A doctor told me that in the middle and senior years lungs are the least exercised organs in the body and that singing in the shower is good for them!

Exercise helps build up the cardiovascular system and prevent the older age difficulty often called "senility." I am convinced that you do not need to succumb to the sunset sickness syndrome with all its aches, pains, losses, and hardened arteries! It is said that Moses lived to be one hundred twenty, yet his eye was not dim nor his natural force abated.

8. Develop the Positive Power Within You

Evelyn Underhill says that "half of the powers of the self are always asleep." [2] Dr. Matthew E. Fairbanks writes, "It's easy to get into the chronic pattern of thinking negatively." [3] Now, put the spotlight on what you *can* do, instead of capitulating to a helplessness attributed to advancing age. Intimidated by "can't," you become a sniveling weakling and a crybaby. Can't makes "can't" people. Can makes "can" people!

I read about a young man in New Jersey who had an accident as a youngster which dislocated his spine. As a result, he had a big hump on his back, for which he had to wear a steel brace. When he entered a private school, he had to get a physical examination. There were many boys waiting in the doctor's office. He looked at them and thought, "I wish I had a strong, straight body like all the others here." When they were told to undress and slip on robes, the young man became terrified because he had never undressed in the presence of others. More importantly, he was embarrassed and ashamed of the hump on his back. Self-deprecation flooded his mind. All he could think about was the hump.

In a few minutes, it was his turn to see the doctor. "Hello, Joseph," the doctor greeted him. "I'm so glad to get to know you. Take the robe off so I can examine you." "The hump," thought Joseph. "He will see my hump." The doctor walked over and pressed his fingers on both sides of Joseph's throat. Through his lighted gadget, he looked into his ears. "Say 'ah,'" the doctor said. He put his stethoscope to the boy's chest, then placed it in the pit of his stomach and told him to breathe deeply. Then the doctor looked into the eyes of the scared boy as he said, "Do you trust in God?"

"Yes, sir," answered Joseph.

"Good," said the doctor. "There's nothing we can do in this world alone. The more faith we have in him, the greater the faith we have in ourselves."

Briskly, the doctor jotted something on Joseph's record, then said, "Pardon me for a moment. I'll be back."

"I wonder what the doctor wrote?" the boy thought. "Probably that I have a big hump on my back." Inquisitively, he walked over to the desk and looked at the record. Under the heading, "Physical Characteristics," he saw, "Has an unusually well-shaped head." That was all! "Has an unusually well-shaped head." [4]

Joseph became a new fellow! By turning his attention from a big hump on the back to "an unusually well-shaped head," which, by no mistake, is what the discerning physician had in mind, he began to develop the positive power within him.

The following are ways to develop your positive power:

1) *Spotlight your abilities rather than your handicaps.* The calamitous middle-aged mindset of "I can't. I'm forty-five!" must be subdued. The youth-oriented Madison Avenue advertising machines and erroneous assessment of capabilities have inflicted on the middle-aged crowd a pathetic inferiority complex. A wrinkleless face and beautiful body have been substituted for the irreplaceable values of knowledge and experience. An energetic employee of solid ability—one who had taken the worst territory in the company and made it the best—once talked with me because he had not been adequately rewarded by his company. I mentioned the possibility of a job change. He exclaimed, "Me! I just turned forty!"

H. G. Wells said it succinctly: "Wealth, notoriety, place, and power are no measure of success whatever. The only true measure of success is the ratio between what we might have done and what we might have been, on the one hand, and the thing we have made of ourselves, on the other." [5]

2) *Begin to laugh at troubles.* Someone assured me that, in this way, we'll never run out of things to laugh at. It won't lessen the size of the problem, but it will better enable you to handle it. Like changing a baby's diaper, it won't permanently solve the problem, but it will make things more endurable for awhile.

3) *Go to school everyday.* Lulled to sleep by indifference, years can bring on a putrifying arrogance, a "know-it-all" and "expert-on-most-everything" attitude. Middle-agers are prone to suffer from what I call "mental-sclerosis"—a hardening

of the intellectual, scholastic, learning arteries. Yet a closed mind is a contradiction. Very little ever goes in, but lots of things are forever coming out.

You need to keep running a stream of ideas. At the tail-end of the middle years, Robert Hearin, the Chairman of the Board for one of the South's leading banks, told me that the possibility of a new deal each day keeps excitement in his professional life. Don't be sluggish in discarding worn-out, useless, no-longer-productive-and-meaningful ideas. Put into effect a personal sunset law on ideas and activities because the quickest way to become an old dog is to quit learning new tricks.

9. Maintain a Hopeful Outlook on Life

As the years march on, people are apt to become cynical, doubtful, gloomy, and negative—claiming, of course, the realities of life. As a man said, "What do you expect after the socks and knocks of life?" Pessimism edges in. A forty-eight year old man I know has a card in his billfold which reads, "I'm a pessimist. In case of accident, I'm not surprised."

When this happens, feelings are affected. Fatigue has a field day. Routine routes the person. There may be drastic effects on the body as pointed out by an article from Associated Press. "Loneliness and estrangement from family may one day be listed . . . as causes of cancer. Studies have confirmed what medical authorities have been saying for centuries. That is, human emotions can be a factor in the development of cancer, just as they are in peptic ulcers, heart ailment, headaches and some other maladies." The source is Johns Hopkins University Medical School where research on this particular subject began thirty years ago.[6]

Dr. Jay Lefer of the New York Medical College called it a "psychobiological process."[7] By no means is every cancer patient one whose outlook on life has been dreary. But scientists have ventured to say that a negative frame of mind— brought on by the loss of a loved one, repression of distasteful childhood experiences, anxiety, fear, stress, or the lack of close relationships—can interfere with the body's ability to prevent disease.

Dr. Joyce Brothers, the psychologist and newspaper columnist, once received a letter which read:

> I'm forty-five and terrified of growing old and senile. I'm so frightened of this that I often fantasize suicide or some accident that will make it unnecessary for me to reach old age. I can't seem to rid myself of this preoccupation, even though I know it's unhealthy.

Dr. Brothers's reply assured the writer that he is not alone. "Because of many myths about aging, many persons have great fears about growing old." She advised, "One reason it's important to change your attitudes now is that these fears, if unchecked, tend to become self-fulfilling. . . . Most individuals can continue to learn new things as long as they live. A positive, optimistic attitude toward life can not only increase longevity, but decrease the likelihood of senility." [8]

Here are some suggestions for holding on to a hopeful outlook:

1) *Keep before you how important you are to your Creator, God.* This will counteract the middle-aged feeling of declining significance.

2) *Intermingle with younger people.* There has been effort to separate the ages. To wit, retirement centers which provide little or no interaction among those of various ages. A man at a huge retirement complex in California told me that all he sees is the hearse coming to pick up his neighbors. Separation builds walls, not bridges. *Each age needs the other age*—to see things in a broader perspective, to have a better understanding of life. Younger people possess bundles of ideas and are brimming with enthusiasm. The realism and idealism of the two groups need the exposure to one another.

3) *Listen to those older than you.* In society and the church, we have taken older people for granted. I overheard a conversation between three waitresses in their twenties and thirties, I'd judge, which demonstrates the problem. One said, "I'd rather stay young than get old, and dried-up, and a no-

body." "Yes," replied another, "and no one listens to you."

There must be an awakening to the genuine significance and importance of our elders. They are persons, too! They are worthwhile, too! They have enormous wisdom, energies, and abilities to offer, too! Furthermore, *the* quality of a person and a society is reflected by the attitude toward, relationship to, and treatment of older persons.

Your connection with your elders now influences what kind of person you are and the way others will think of you, relate to you, and treat you when you are older. Joseph Addison, the seventeenth-century English essayist, put it this way: "He who would pass his declining years with honor and comfort, should, when young, consider that he may one day become old, and remember when he is old, that he has once been young." [9]

4) *Be open to new ways of doing things.* In middle age, we tend to adopt a rigid, inflexible set of actions. It's the same old way, day after day. New methods are avoided. Honest surprises come few and far between. The fun is squashed out of activities. Then we are no longer fun to be with and know.

5) *Take no one for granted,* neither your marriage partner, nor friends, nor business associates, nor fellow workers. If you do take people for granted, courtesies diminish and show of appreciation shrinks. Some of the romance sinks out of life. Do not take your job for granted; do not think, "Well, I have been here fifteen years, so I rate." When this happens, performance suffers, professional value slides.

6) *Be willing to take considered risks.* Super-cautious people suffer an element of mental death. "Change jobs? Change my personality at my age? No-sir, I've got to protect." Fine, but petrify—no! Playing it too safe can be a hazard!

10. Start Letting Others Help You

Probably you have taken pride in your ability to be independent. In a sense, this is natural. One of the fears of the middle and older years is dependence. But a fierce desire to remain independent whatever the sacrifice is not good. To some of us who attended a Mississippi Conference on Problems of the Retired and Aged, Dr. Robert Soileau of Louisiana State University said, "The concept of retirement as a time to be spent waiting for death is a primitive one that has been and must continue to be challenged." Dr. Soileau noted that a weakness of America's work ethic is that it encourages retired persons to consider themselves useless, to feel shame and guilt when faced with an unstructured life and time and energy to spend as they wish. He said, "This guilt hinders many retired persons in their search for new roles, and it shames many who need assistance into refusing to accept it."

Gerald Schomp writes, "Thousands of senior citizens . . . have never made peace with old age. They live in loneliness, in despair, seeking comfort out of a bottle, narcoticizing themselves into a hazy stupor. Little is being done about this problem, because these old people have little motivation to seek help or accept it when it is offered. These defeated people have failed to find meaning for the remaining years of their lives." [10]

Usually, the need for help increases with age. It may be that you will become totally dependent in later years, and that will be okay if it is an honest dependency. The truth is:

> You are really independent *only* when you are willing to lean on others when necessary.

> You can *give* help only to the extent that you are willing to receive help.

A good word here is *interdependence*—a dependence on one another. Here's how to practice interdependence:

1) *Welcome the new opportunity to be interdependent or even dependent.* Don't suppress or repress the chance!

2) *Turn interdependence into a blessing of togetherness.*

3) *Show appreciation for help,* at least a sincere "thank you, it is thoughtful of you to help me."

4) *Offer your assistance to someone who needs it.* Make it a two-way street. Totally dependent on others, a paraplegic with whom I am acquainted lets his helpers know that he is

thinking good thoughts about them and remembering them in prayer.

In the middle years, you are free to make your choices. You can choose the path you will take in approaching retirement. But once the choices are made and carried out to their conclusion, you are no longer free to choose the consequences of those choices. Therefore, whether retirement years are a miracle or a morgue can be largely determined *now!* This is the time to make intelligent, promising choices for years to come.

3.

Half As Much Money

*"The great use of life is to spend it
for something that outlasts it."*
—*William James*

I have defined retirement as a cessation from the vocational activity on which you depended for livelihood. It is a colossal step, to be sure, and one which casts on you nine dominant needs:

1) *Adequate finances:* Having enough to enjoy life; making it on what you have, and getting the most out of what you have!

2) *Health Care:* You live in a day when costs have risen one thousand percent, when the average stay in the hospital costs $1,300.00—$170.00 per day! At this time, expenses for health are continuing to go up.

3) *Companionship:* A growing relationship with your spouse, then someone to help meet the shock of single living after the spouse dies. Or people to be with if you have always been single.

4) *Personal dignity:* You need to enjoy a genuine sense of self-worth in older years and the feeling that "I'm still somebody!"

5) *Integration into society:* You must still be a part of society, and not a "has-been," a "castoff," or a fifth wheel!

6) *Meaningful activities:* Take advantage of your experience and potential! Express your abilities in creative ways! Combat loneliness and boredom, two of the biggest problems people confront in older years!

7) *Living facilities:* They need to be adequate enough to meet your needs and as beautiful as possible to encourage life, not death.

8) *Wholesome attitudes:* This is a frame of mind sufficient enough to meet life as an older person and to deal with disabilities and infirmities!

9) *Spiritual wholeness:* Inner vibrancy for living *and* dying so that you are enabled to live a fuller life and accept dying as an act of God's love and grace.

One of the sharpest realities of retirement living is reduced resources. A retired man complained, "If only I had more money." For a large number of retirees, the cry is the same. But is this not true throughout life? Marriage counselors have found that the most common reason for marital problems given by people of all ages is shortage of money. "We don't have enough to make it."

Finances are not everything, but they are a big something. Dr. Paul Tournier, the respected Swiss author, wrote, "Life changes entirely if a retired person enjoys a certain measure of financial ease, even a modest one, instead of having to count every penny and to go without everything except what is required merely to subsist." [1]

Along this line, money is necessary for some leisure activities like reading (when you must purchase books), certain hobbies, gardening, and travel. Then there are medical care and friends and loved ones whom you want to remember with a gift from time to time.

A good rule of thumb to apply during retirement years is that you need about half as much money as you made at the peak of your employment years. This is assuming that mortgages are either paid or greatly reduced.

On what do you spend it? According to U.S. government reports on the use of the retirement dollar, the average couple spends it as follows:

Housing	35¢
Food	26¢

Clothing and Personal Expenses	9¢
Transportation	9¢
Medical Care	9¢
Contributions	6¢
Other	6¢

I want to impress upon you six principles of money management in retirement years:

SIX PRINCIPLES OF MONEY MANAGEMENT IN RETIREMENT YEARS

1. Move From Making Money to Using It

You have invested forty or so years in making money. Time, effort, abilities, energy, and ingenuity have been exchanged for spendable cash. Now, in retirement, it is time to spend it. Stockpiling is no longer necessary.

"Spending won't be hard," a couple said, "with no more than we have." Possibly you are in the same boat. Still, the emphasis is the same. Use what you have, but use it wisely.

Another man, in his seventies, had accumulated a comfortable estate. He was urged by his son to use the money. "After all, Dad," the son reasoned, "you can't take it with you." The father replied, "Then I won't go." Of course, every one of us is going to "go" sooner or later. No one actually has any assurance of breath beyond the present one!

There is a story about a man who vowed to take his money with him. Somehow a Brink's armored truck was caught in the middle of his funeral procession. When the line of vehicles passed through his neighborhood, someone exclaimed, "By george, he *is* taking it with him!"

No, you won't and can't. I am basically in agreement with the action taken by the man whose last will and testament was read to relatives. "Being of sound mind, I spent it all while I was living."

Your Primary Responsibility
Is to Your Own Well-Being

You may possess more than enough to adequately care for yourself. Then it is reasonable to remember loved ones and friends. But keep in mind that each generation needs the blessings which come from standing on its own feet. If you must scrimp and skip to provide for your own needs, your loved ones and friends should enthusiastically endorse the philosophy "spend it while you're living."

But there is a problem in getting the tide turned from making money to using it. In a previous chapter, I mentioned a certain continuity to life which goes with a person from one stage to another. If you have been overzealous in your efforts to accumulate money, a pattern has developed that will be tough to change.

I recall the gentleman whose entire life had been wrapped up in making money. He honestly enjoyed accumulating as much of it as possible. By his own admission, he had become a skinflint over a thirty-year period. Although he was worth several million dollars, he lived like a common laborer. Well into retirement years, he still relished piling up money. Why, his income from investments alone was in the six-figure bracket! Recognizing the trap in which he had grown, he said, "I can't change! I should! God, I wish I could! But I can't!"

Alexander Pope, the eighteenth-century English poet, outlined the tragedy succinctly. "When we are young, we are slavishly employed in procuring something whereby we may live comfortably when we grow old; and when we are old, we perceive it is too late to live as we proposed." Sir William Temple, the seventeenth-century statesman, added, "There cannot live a more unhappy creature than an ill-natured old man, who is neither capable of receiving pleasures, nor sensible of conferring them on others." [2]

Not only is it okay to change this pattern, but it is desirable —it is a necessity! Even though you have waited until retirement, the habit can be altered and changed.

2. Don't Fill Your Retirement Years with Rainy Days

One of the most common statements I hear from older people is, "I'm saving for a rainy day." Or, "I can't do this, that, or the other, because at my age, I might break my hip and have to go to the hospital." Consciously or unconsciously, catastrophe seems to always lurk behind the next corner.

Saving is all right; however, it should no longer be required or expected. Furthermore, how many rainy days can a person have? It is time to enjoy the fruit of your laboring years! Oh, to be sure, a person is wise to have an emergency fund available, but it needs to be realistic, reasonable, and a helpmate to the joy of living *today*.

3. Prepare for the Distribution of Resources Remaining at Your Death

The last human eventuality is not death, but the distribution of estate *after* a person dies. To do this is a responsible act of the living and a positive response to human need.

The responsibility for the use of material blessings accumulated on this side of the grave is on your hands. A person dies, yet he can still live on by preparation for an orderly and thoughtful disposition of his worldly goods.

Ask yourself, "Why give family, business associates, and others the chance to fight over the results of my genius, work, and plans?" To allow these blessings of a lifetime—perhaps several generations—to be swallowed up in legal fees and taxes is an abuse and misuse of intelligence. Consultation with a tax expert, an attorney, and representatives of church and favorite charities or colleges is a smart move.

4. Take Advantage of Available Opportunities

A person does not have to spend a sizable amount of money to enjoy the retirement years. Your resources may be limited or you may have plenty of money to provide for every convenience. Still, the following services can add to your leisure years:

1) *Church activities:* Special programs, luncheons, outings, and projects may be available at little or no charge to you.

2) *Community clubs and organizations for older persons:* These can be a source of real meaning, friendship, and mutual endeavor at little or no cost to you.

3) *Reading:* By checking out books and magazines from your local library, you can span the world of science, geography, philosophy, and fiction from your own living room!

4) *Walks:* This will improve your health and expose you to the outdoors and other people. All it takes is time—and you have plenty of time—mixed in with a little effort.

5) *Rides:* Even with gasoline prices as high as they are, it is still a bargain to take short trips, or extended ones, and enjoy the beauty, uniqueness, and people of other communities.

6) *Legal services:* Probably there is a group in your own community which offers legal assistance either at no charge or little cost to retirees.

7) *Tax services:* Taxes are certain, but tax laws are changing constantly. Perhaps as many as one-half of older persons pay more taxes than necessary. Seek out assistance where you live.

8) *Special discounts:* Some banks offer reduced rates to older persons. Lower rates may be available from various businesses. Some drugstores cut up to twenty percent off prescription drugs for retirees. Free or low-cost transportation may be available in your area. Possibly there is housing at bargain prices for older persons in the area, especially for those on the lower income scale.

9) *Recreational areas:* There are some which give a break to retirees. Seeking out these places could mean money, fun, and more enjoyment for your life.

10) *Government services:* They include Medicare, Medicaid, Food Stamps, Home Meals, Community Meals, Home Care Services, and Supplemental Security Income. Check with the city office in your area or the Social Security office.

5. Watch the Use of Charge Accounts

It is very easy to use credit cards and accounts and there are many of them available. But credit with such ease can become a pain on the brain and a drain on the pocketbook! As an older person said, "How can I ever pay these bills? I didn't know I'd bought so much!"

Unless paid within twenty-five or thirty days, most cards and accounts add a generous eighteen-to-thirty-percent interest per annum. Some have even begun to tag on a convenient service charge for each time they are used so that people who pay within the interest-free period will nevertheless pay for the use of the card. I know of a company whose fee is fifty cents a charge.

A retired man told me about some advice his father gave him. Never charge anything that is consumable and perishable! That is an intelligent rule of thumb. Also, keep up with your charges. If you are on a strict budget, use the credit card only when it is absolutely necessary. And pay the bill within the interest-free period.

6. Make It on What You Have Available

I am convinced that many middle-aged and older persons have more than what they think, or know, or admit. This happens when financial ability is measured only by the amount of spendable cash available instantly. In fact, many have other assets which can be translated into spendable funds.

On the other hand, some older persons have little more than what the meager Social Security check totals each month. Regardless, it is necessary to determine what you have. To do this, first list the sources of your income:

Monthly Income

Social Security	$_____
Interest from Savings	$_____
Earnings from Investments	$_____

Pension Plan $_____

Annuity $_____

Income from Insurance $_____

Other $_____

TOTAL $_____

Now, list your expenses:

Fixed Expenses

Church and Other
Charitable Gifts $_____

Rent or Mortgage $_____

Taxes $_____

Insurance $_____

Membership Dues $_____

Loans or Other Debts $_____

Deposit to Emergency Fund $_____

Other $_____

TOTAL $_____

Adjustable Expenses

Food $_____

Medical $_____

Utilities $_____

Clothing $_____

Automobile $_____

Recreation $_____

Gifts (birthdays,
anniversaries, etc.) $_____

Other $_____

TOTAL $_____

Finally, subtract your total income from your total expenses:

GRAND TOTAL EXPENSES	$_____
GRAND TOTAL INCOME	-$_____
DIFFERENCE	$_____

If the expenses are greater than income, can you reasonably make adjustments? Also, what are some additional sources? One is *part-time work*. I know a wonderful woman in her seventies who sews for pleasure and profit. My father is in his early seventies. For as long as I can remember, he has enjoyed gardening. Six months out of the year during my childhood, we ate items grown in the garden. And we always seemed to have the most beautiful yard on the block. Now he still does some gardening; for him it is a source of additional income, enjoyment, and creative expression.

Another possible source of income is the *principal* of savings and investments. Perhaps you have no problem taking the interest, but why not use some of the principal along the way? On the day my Granddad Ray died, he had a bank balance of eighty-four cents, but he had been self-sufficient for the twenty years of his retirement!

Still another source of income is *family*—at least, it should be! There is a moral, social, and spiritual responsibility for the younger members of a family—and older ones, too, if they have the resources—to assist elderly relatives in need. Help from the government and from organizations which have a concern for retired people is good, but the first line of help should come from the family. St. Paul wrote, "If a widow has children or grandchildren, let them first learn their religious duty to their own family and make some return to their parents; for this is acceptable in the sight of God" (1 Tim. 5:4, RSV). He also instructed, "If any one does not provide for his relatives, and especially for his own family, he has disowned the faith and is worse than an unbeliever" (1 Tim. 5:8, RSV).

This spirit of family responsibility can never be broken. It has often been shirked in a modern society where family ties have generally deteriorated. Often the state is expected to shoulder the need. Although the state does have a certain amount of responsibility, it is secondary to that of the family. In my family, the need to support older relatives has never arisen. Nevertheless, my wife and I made a mutual commitment years ago that family assistance, if and when needed, is not optional for us.

Some friends of mine help their retired parents. Even ten or fifteen dollars a month makes the difference some retired family members need. There are some children who have banded together to pool twenty or twenty-five dollars a month each for their needy parents and grandparents. That's the spirit! *That's the obligation!* The bond of love and emotional reinforcement reflected by family support is probably as important as the dollars.

To make it on what money you have available, the key word is management. Without intelligent and disciplined management, it hardly makes much difference whether a person's retirement income is two thousand or fifteen thousand a year. The excuse will still be, "If I only had more money."

I am acquainted with a woman whose Social Security income totaled less than two hundred dollars a month. She had no family and, because of a disability, she was unable to work. But the many local, state, and national government services, such as food stamps, supplemental income, Medicare, and rent subsidy, eased the load significantly. Properly budgeted, her check would have met the rest of her primary needs. But within four days after she received it, the money was spent. When she asked for help, I recommended some concerned women who were willing to help her plan and budget. She refused, claiming, "I don't need them."

Face this question honestly: *"Is my problem a lack of money or the management of the money I do have?"* By determining how much you need and how much you have, you can begin to pull the difference together. Seek the counsel of a competent individual, someone who is willing to help you organize and budget your resources.

Most of all, set your mind to make it on what is available. Epicurus, the ancient Greek philosopher, wisely advised, "It is impossible to live pleasurably without living prudently, and honorably, and justly; or to live prudently, and honorably, and justly, without living pleasurably." [3]

4.

Geritol to Demerol—
Or Is There a Better Way?

"There are no diseases of the aged,
simply diseases among the aged."
—*American Medical Association*

The prescription for health care among some older persons ranges from snorts of Geritol to shots of Demerol. I remember the man in his sixties who occasionally went to the doctor for a shot of Demerol. "Oh," I inquired, "you must suffer intense pain." He replied, "No, it's not for pain. At least, not the pain you're thinking about." When I asked the reason, he explained, "For twenty-four hours, it drowns the hurt in my heart."

Health is a major concern of older persons and it should be. *Health is better than wealth!* God gives you the body you have with its ten trillion cells. But we must now admit that health is not restricted to the physical frame. My friend and his Demerol shots pungently point out that boredom, worry, a sense of hopelessness and loneliness, and self-minimization directly influence the physical well-being of a person. Conversely, the state of the body directly affects emotional and mental well-being. Tryon Edwards, the nineteenth-century American clergyman and author, expressed keen insight into the interplay between mind and body. "Age does not depend upon years, but upon temperament and health." [1]

The myth about aging and illness must be dispelled once and for all. Most diseases are *not* synonymous with getting older, although stress and sickness can accelerate an aging syndrome. Let's consider cerebral blood flow and oxygen consumption, for instance. Tests have proven that there is no significant difference between normal, healthy twenty-one year old men and healthy men between ages sixty-five and ninety! This is not all. Older persons who are physically, emotionally, and mentally healthy tend to think more effectively than younger people because they have a vast inventory of experience on which to draw. The older person is more inclined to think in terms of a concept than in a series of details.[2]

Hopefully, Horace Walpole, the eighteenth-century English author, was kidding when he stated, "Since I must be old and have the gout, I have long turned those disadvantages to my own account, and plead them to the utmost when they will save me from doing anything I dislike." [3] The error comes when aging is equated with illness. Most illnesses attributed to age are no respecters of age! In the following pages I suggest Ten Healthful Helpers that can contribute to a better state of body and mind.

TEN HEALTHFUL HELPERS

1. Get a Thorough Physical Checkup Every Six Months

Preventive health care can be a great boon to your total well-being. It can save money, time in bed and hospital, energy, and unnecessary emotional trauma. You will not avoid dying, but you can delay it in a meaningful way. And you can really enjoy the delay. The checkup should include these points, at least:

1) *EKG* (electro-cardiogram).
2) *Complete X-rays.*
3) *Blood chemistry evaluation.*
4) *Urine and stool tests.*
5) *Blood pressure reading.*
6) *Pap smear and breast examination (for women).*

When medicine is prescribed, take it. One of the problems faced by physicians is getting patients to stick to their medicine for as long as they need it. At times you may feel like the person who said in one of my seminars, "I'm so full of penicillin that if I sneeze, someone here is bound to get well." Don't take what you don't need, but take what you need as long as you need it. Your doctor is the expert. Work with him.

2. Eat Nutritious Foods

After twenty years, I saw Bill, a high school friend. To my surprise, he weighed the same as he had when he was eighteen. I said, "You look like there's been a famine in West Texas." Bill replied, "And you look like you caused it!"

Fatty foods and excessive calorie intake cause the problem. Overweight occurs when you eat more than the body actually needs. The surplus turns into rolls of fat around the stomach and spare chins. Such conditions cause a sluggish, tired feeling and a slowing of mental processes. Remember: The ideal weight in retirement years is what you weighed when you were twenty-five (assuming you were not overweight then!) This scale requires a thirty percent reduction in calorie consumption.

The answer is a nutritious menu which reduces calorie intake. A high-protein breakfast launches the day off to a much better start. Other meals need to include a sufficient supply of calcium.

Here are some suggestions for maintaining a healthful diet:

1) *Consult your physician or public health care center for copies of menus which will guide you to healthful eating.* The broad selection of food will surprise you. And you will discover that eating nutritiously can be fun and interesting.

2) *Don't be afraid to augment your menu with a vitamin pill each day.*

3) *See if there is a government-sponsored hot-meal program in your community.* In some areas, this program is held five days each week. The meals are nutritious and well-balanced. Usually, they are served in group dining rooms, like the fellowship hall of a church, and transportation may be provided. The program is available both to people of limited

income and to those who are not financially strapped. Those who are able pay what they can afford, but not in excess of a very reasonable rate. Of course, the fellowship with other people adds to the value of the program.

4) *If you are confined to your house and are unable to prepare food, your community may have a "meals-on-wheels" program.* I know of churches which are agents of this worthy service. The cost is determined by your ability to pay, but not an amount more than a fair cost. For information, call Allied Services in your area or City Hall.

5) *You may be eligible for food stamps.* They can be used for meals sponsored by the government as well as to buy groceries for nutritious eating.

6) *Evaluate and plan—those are the key words.* You may need to make changes in your eating habits. Plan your menu a week in advance. This will help you to intelligently shop; it will minimize impulsive buying.

3. Get Adequate Body Exercise

Regular exercise squeezes the veins and pushes blood toward the heart. This gives the circulatory system, which is a source of problems for many older persons, a needed workout. Daily exercise helps keep body weight and blood pressure down. It reinforces the cardiovascular system and helps prevent senility. Even the aging syndrome is slowed down. For example, young people who are confined to bed and unable to exercise begin to age physiologically. Dr. Tenley Albright, a surgeon, says, "My medical experience has proven one thing to me: the more physically fit people are, the better they respond to treatment. Active people handle pain and injury better than inactive ones." [4]

Physical exercise may be the oldest and best tranquilizer. Dr. Fairbanks writes, "It provides the perfect outlet for the accumulated frustrations, anxieties, and tensions of everyday living. It also improves the quality of your sleep." [5]

Dr. Walter E. O'Donnell, a physician, points out that exercise is an energy booster. He writes about a woman with a

high-pressure job. At the end of the day, she often is totally
drained physically and emotionally. "When that happens,"
she said, "I drag myself home and jog a couple of miles before
starting dinner. It's the last thing in the world I feel like
doing, but it really works. I feel much more energy *after*
running than I do before." [6]

George Leonard adds, "You'll have more energy. By exert-
ing energy in a moderate, rhythmic way, you gain energy for
the rest of living." Then, he outlined more healthy by-prod-
ucts which apply to older persons, too.

1. You'll eat less. Regular exercise helps to control the ap-
   petite.
2. Your pulse rate will slow. By raising your heartbeat to
   around one hundred thirty a minute for at least thirty minutes at least three times a week, you increase the efficiency
   of the entire blood and breathing system.
3. You'll possibly stop smoking. Once you start breathing
   freely and fully, you may not want to smoke.
4. Your desire for alcohol will likely diminish.
5. You'll feel better generally, more sensuous, more a part of
   nature. [7]

People your age are actually doing it—Stig Patterson, 40,
Roger Ruth, 44, Richard Morcom, 51, Herbert Schmidt, 61,
Dr. Paul Spangler, 77, Dr. George Sheehan, 58, Ruth Ander-
son, 47, Duncan MacLean, 90, C. Speechley, 87, and Fritz
Schreiber, 80! [8] A. E. Walker, a neighbor of mine, walks
three to four miles a day by going to the end of the street
and back to his yard. The round-trip route is about sixty-five
yards. A heart patient and several years beyond sixty, Mr.
Walker says, "It's good exercise and it keeps the fat off."

Jogging, swimming, bicycling, climbing stairs, and walking
are good exercises. You can also exercise in your own house
and backyard. There are standing, sitting, and lying exercises
which may be best suited for your condition. For example:

1. Sit on the floor and stretch out your legs.
2. Bend your elbows and lean back on your forearms, keeping
   your head up.

3. Raise your legs, bend your knees and bring them toward you, keeping the portion of your legs below your knees in a horizontal position. Point your toes toward the ceiling.

4. Reach for the ceiling with your legs. Straighten them up, vertically. Hold for a ten count.

5. Lower your knees back to the bended position, elevated off the floor.

6. Go through the exercise twenty times.

Your body is a masterful creation capable of taking much more than you have imagined! Here are some suggestions for keeping it in shape

1) *Get the advice of your doctor.* Maybe your visit should include an EKG.

2) *Start exercising at a slower pace and increase a week at a time.* Don't try to conquer Rome in a day!

3) *Do something every day.* The scheme is to build line upon line. The habit will grow on you.

4) *Work up to fifteen minutes a day.* This way, you will eventually invest 105 minutes a week in exercise for healthful living.

5) *Work up to exercises that cause you to sweat.* They will increase your heartbeat and breathing temporarily.

As I mentioned in a previous chapter, I walk up to two miles each night. It takes me fifteen to twenty minutes although I do not rush it. The longer, steady, rhythmic steps move me along at a consistent pace. A man in the neighborhood has been "jogging" for two years. I have seen him pass our house shuffling his feet along, progressing about six inches at a time. I started my walk one evening just as he was "jogging" by the house. When he turned a corner one and one-half blocks down the street, I was nearly a block ahead of the man!

Mini-efforts at exercise as well as wild bursts of sudden, occasional exercises are useless! In addition, they may be dangerous.

6) *Don't be afraid to vary and change exercises.* In fact, some variety stimulates interest and enjoyment. If you become bored with what you are doing, adopt another form for awhile. Some older persons have four or five different methods. They may walk one day, for example, and the next day swim, or play tennis, or bicycle.

4. Get Enough Sleep

Doctors ask, "What's your sleeping pattern? How long do you sleep on an average night?" A deficient amount of sleep can cause health problems.

But there is a parallel question which is just as important. Do you sleep while you are asleep? The rest and renewal which sleep is designed to bring to mind and body can be thwarted. Dr. O'Donnell advised that the solution to shallow, fitful, often-interrupted sleep is not tranquilizers or sleeping pills: "Drugs make your sleep more disturbed in the long run. The only way to break a pattern of insomnia is to seek out the root causes." [9] The following are ways to have restful sleep:

1) *Leave the worries of the day outside your bedroom door.* Place whatever concerns you in God's hands for the night. As a man said to me, "I can sleep in peace. God stays awake."

2) *Over a period of time, daily exercises will prepare you for a night of restful sleep.* The exertion of effort sets mind and body for rest. Some people find, however, that exercise *immediately* before going to bed keeps them awake, and prefer to exercise early in the day.

3) *Before you turn off the light, spend five to ten minutes reading some inspirational or devotional material.* The last conscious act you perform before going to sleep works in your unconscious while you are asleep! Perhaps your fitful night results from watching a chiller, thriller, or killer on TV immediately before going to bed. Set up an inspirational, devotional buffer zone between such stuff and bedtime. This will have a calming effect on you.

4) *Confine your evening eating to a balanced and moderate dinner.* Besides adding another chin, bedtime eating can be detrimental to sleep.

5. Arrange to Be Alone a Few Minutes During the Day

You live in a noisy world, even as an older person. The individual can get caught in a whirl of busy-ness. Although I deal with this subject more adequately in another chapter, let me say here that everyone, whatever his age, needs the therapeutic value which comes from a time of personal aloneness each day.

Dr. Harold A. Blood told thousands of physicians at an annual convention of the American Osteopathic Association, "The stress of modern living arouses a protest from the gastrointestinal system that daily engages the healing arts practitioner and is responsible for millions of dollars being spent annually." As a result, conditions like anxiety, depression, fear, and hypochondria threaten our physical well-being. Fifteen minutes of aloneness *every day* can turn the trick. Here are some ways to make this time work for you:

1) *Get away from the usual routine of your day and be a part of a peaceful surrounding.* You don't necessarily have to go beyond your own house—get in a place by yourself. It is a time when you are alone with your wonderful self.

2) *Make this time count by using meditation.* I practice Christian Meditation which increases my awareness of the presence of God, empowers me to cope better with life and myself, releases me from anxiety, fear, and depression to hope, anticipation, and fuller life, and helps me to uncover and loose the greater potential there is to my life. I recommend Christian Meditation. At any rate, use some method in your quiet time to enlarge your capacity for life.

3) *Think quietly.* Starve disruptive, disturbing thoughts by denying them the spotlight. Bring to mind a scene which is serene and calm.

6. Keep Looking Ahead

One of the problems in older years is to look no further than the immediate moment. On the one hand, this can be good. Not a one of us is guaranteed a minute of life beyond this moment. This is the moment to live! On the other hand, the immediate moment can be defeating and become a partner to the aches and pains of the moment.

You need to always be looking ahead. *Live as if each breath was your last!* Get the most out of the present moment. Give life this moment the best and most you can. But plan as if you will live another year! Looking ahead gives you something at which to aim. Define your life so that you will have activities and plans in front of you. They will pull you forward. Here are some things that may help you look ahead.

1) *Set priorities.* Yes, even at your age it is important to have priorities for the use of time. Otherwise, time flitters away into nothingness. Despair, a sense of futility, uselessness, and ultimate hopelessness creep in. Or, you will probably find that too much of your time is wasted on depreciating trivia. I asked a retired person about his day and he replied, "TV!" It had become the sum of his life. A widow shared, "By establishing my priorities, I have been pulled to my children and grandchildren, painting, gardening, and church activities. My life is much more exciting!"

2) *Plan something for tomorrow that has promise of adding meaning to your life.* For example, a trip to the zoo, theater, or a concert. Make it something of which you can unashamedly claim, "I am planning this to benefit *me!*"

3) *Plan something for tomorrow which will benefit another person.* A phone call to a friend, a visit with a lonely person, a letter to a loved one, a pie for a neighbor, some project at the church or club. Make it something of which you can proudly say, "I am planning this to benefit *another person!*"

4) *Plan something major three months, six months, and*

twelve months ahead. I know people in their seventies and eighties who are planning trips a year in advance.

5) *Follow through with your plans.* Naturally, they need to be realistic and challenging. Your plans must not be impossible. Then, act on your plans unless a serious development in the meanwhile hinders you. Accept things the way they are, but don't allow the insignificant to gun down these plans!

7. Practice Surmountability Thinking

You have heard that life begins at forty. When you consider the experience of four hundred famous people, you may choose to believe that life begins at sixty! Each of the four hundred was the most outstanding statesman, painter, military leader, poet, businessman, or writer of his time. Each realized his greatest achievements after he passed age sixty! Thirty-five percent of those achievements came between sixty and seventy; twenty-three percent between seventy and eighty; and eight percent were over eighty! Sixty percent of their most outstanding work was done when they were beyond sixty! [10]

After he was seventy years of age, Vanderbilt constructed most of his railroads! Michelangelo sculpted masterfully at eighty-nine! Monet painted his best pictures after he was eighty-five! Harlan Sanders, the Colonel of Kentucky Fried Chicken fame, started the business after he was sixty-five! Palmerston was the Premier of England at eighty-one; Gladstone at eighty-three! These words may be familiar to you:

> For tho' from out our bourne of Time and Place
>   The flood may bear me far,
> I hope to see my Pilot face to face,
>   When I have crossed the bar. [11]

They are from Alfred Lord Tennyson's "Crossing The Bar"—one of the most quoted poems from his vast repertoire. He was eighty-three when he penned them!

An older person reminded me, "But I'm not a Tennyson, Gladstone, Sanders, or Michelangelo." He was right. Neither

are you, for your Creator made you a unique person. You
are you! Yet you have in you some of the spirit which made
Tennyson, Sanders, and company. At least, you have the capacity.

But they possessed a common denominator. I call it Surmountability Thinking. Instead of thinking, "I'm over the hill
and I can't do anything," they thought, "I'm still a person of
possibilities and I will try to use them." Such thinking is non-
discriminatory except as it is self-imposed. On your level,
where you are, and to your life, you can practice Surmountability Thinking, an accessory to more therapeutic living.
Here are some aspects of Surmountability Thinking:

1) *When you face a problem, ask, "How will I overcome
it?"* Some older people wonder, "Can I overcome my problem?" "Can" implies doubt as to whether it is possible to
handle the difficulty. The question I propose assumes the
problem can be overcome. The quest becomes finding a way.

2) *Say "thanks" for happenings in your life.* This does not
mean that everything which happens is good, but it does
mean that, in some way, something good can be squeezed out
of everything which happens. This thankful spirit will enable
you to better accept, cope with, and handle those happenings.

3) *Start saying thanks for little things.* There is a corre-
sponding connection between an attitude of gratitude and
what a person thinks can be done. The way to develop the
spirit of gratefulness is to verbalize your appreciation for
small things.

4) *Think on the happier side.* A depressed person suffers
a slowing down of his metabolic processes. Gloomitis kills
people! A physician told me that if he could be absolutely
honest in his report as to the cause of death for a patient, he
would write "Gloomitis." "The man could be alive and on
the road to recovery, but he gave in to gloom."

5) *When you tend to wallow in self-pity, do something
good for someone or say some good word to someone, quick!*
An overdose of self-centeredness is destructive. Break out of
its shell by a simple expression of interest in another person.
Besides, this will help you to feel happier with yourself.

6) *Challenge yourself by taking on an extraordinary project occasionally.* It needs to be something which will test your supreme abilities and resources. Then follow through on it to a successful conclusion.

7. *Affirm the potential with which God has endowed you.* The Bible summed it up in these words: "I can do all things in him who strengthens me" (Phil. 4:13, RSV). Applied individually, it means that you can do what your God wants you to do.

8. Renew Relationships

Older people are healthier when they have meaningful relationships. There is a sense of acceptance and being loved and appreciated when you enjoy a happy relationship with other people that combats the creeping tendency toward isolation. Here are some suggestions:

1) *Be the initiator of a growing relationship with your family.* Love and goodwill are important ingredients, but remember that love is more than a feeling. Love is an act and word in behalf of another. When a feeling of love is absent, you can still love by acting and talking in a loving way.

2) *Rebuild a relationship which has deteriorated.* It is not a question of who takes the first step; the need is to rebuild. When you are aware of the need, you are responsible for doing what is within your power to resurrect it from the ashes.

3) *Make an effort to develop new friends.* Through relocation and death, retirement removes some close friends. One man lamented, "Those who were dear to me have either died or moved." In resignation, he had begun to surrender his God-given claim on life until he started to make new friends. Life for him started anew. Your church and social clubs are excellent resources for friendships. Casual talks with neighbors may lead to mutually satisfying friendships.

4) *Maintain contact with established friends.* Write letters and make a few long-distance phone calls to your friends who have moved away. Include in your travels stop-overs with them. Visit those who are in the area.

9. Maintain an Easy Flow in Life

Demands (at least, what you think are demands), expectations, and the pressures of older age gang up on you. They can corner you and result in ulcers, high blood pressure, strokes, or coronaries. According to Dr. John Cassel, Chairman of the Department of Epidemiology at the University of North Carolina, and Dr. Curtis Hames, a Georgia physician, such occurrences are less likely to happen to some people.

These two doctors headed a ten-year study which involved every resident of Evans County, Georgia, over forty years of age, plus half of those who were between fifteen and thirty-nine years of age. In all, 3,102 persons were a part of the study. The doctors outline the number-one factor for those with better health in this phrase: "They approached their life with a sense of equanimity, something that helps prolong their lives. [We] were impressed with their ability to do this, even when confronted with catastrophic situations." [12] I have listed some ways to help maintain an attitude of equanimity.

1) *Don't take yourself too seriously.* Benjamin Franklin captured the idea in older age when he said, "I'm in the prime of my senility." [13] You are a human being. Human beings have weaknesses and faults. Instead of letting them bury you, rise above them. Laugh at silly mistakes and go on living.

2) *Don't take things too seriously.* Anything which happens to you has happened to others. Probably the same thing is happening to many thousands of people at the same time it is happening to you. Therefore, you are not alone; any feeling you have has been felt by others. At the time you feel it, probably thousands of people are feeling the same way. This happening and feeling can be a bomb or a bridge, depending on *you*.

3) *Relax a little everyday.* "Relax" means "to loose from." It is to be less tense, unwound, less nervous. Older people have a favorite malady—a "case of nerves." In reality, it is tension. As young people say, "You're uptight." The literal truth is contained in that statement. The person is mentally and, as a result, muscularly tied-up. Parts of the body reply

with tightness; for instance, the back, neck, and upper pit of the stomach. The consequences may include nausea, headaches, and pain in the neck. Prolonged tenseness is a first-class ticket to sickness! Without any relief, tension accumulates. Take a few minutes each day to consciously relax and you will experience rewarding dividends.

10. Use Available Medical Services

Why is it that older people hesitate to seek professional help in times of physical and emotional need? Possibly the reasons include the idea that visits will cost a fortune, the fear of hospitalization, and the feeling that they don't have the strength to get to a doctor's office. If funds are limited, they may think they will be a burden on society. "Disgraceful!" insisted one person in this condition. "I will not become a charity case!"

When it comes to an emotional need, there seems to be a strong social pressure. "What would my friends think?" "Me go to a psychologist or psychiatrist? You've got to be kidding."

These self-inflicted restrictions need to be dissolved because you, as a person, are valuable! *Your worth is immeasurably great!* Therefore, your well-being is of basic importance.

As we discussed in an earlier chapter, a radical independence is just as detrimental and immoral as the idea that "society owes me a living." You are responsible for doing what you are honestly capable of doing. If this comes up short, then others should be given the opportunity to make up the difference:

1) *When in need of transportation to the doctor, contact a loved one, neighbor, your church, or the city.* Keep in mind that your feeling of reluctance to request help is probably the biggest degree of reluctance felt by anyone.

2) *Be willing to use Medicare and Medicaid.* Medicare is health insurance available from the government through the local Social Security office. You must be sixty-five years or over to qualify and be registered at Social Security. It is ad-

visable to register at least three months prior to your sixty-fifth birthday. If you are under sixty-five and disabled, you may qualify for some Medicare benefits. Check into it.

Part A of Medicare pays a substantial amount of hospital care. It also covers some health services necessary after you leave the hospital. Although this coverage is free to you, it does not cover all hospital costs.

Part B of Medicare pays a portion of doctors' fees, therapy, and related supplies and services. But it is not necessary for you to be hospitalized to receive these benefits. When you apply for Part A, you are enrolled in Part B. Part B requires a minimum payment each month. Understand that Medicare does not pay all costs and there are some expenses it does not cover at all.

Consequently, you may need to get some supplemental health insurance. Your place of employment may have a group plan. See whether it covers retired employees. If not, you still may be able to convert it to an individual policy. There are supplemental plans available which help to fill in for deficiencies of Medicare.

Medicaid is especially for those who are unable to pay for Medicare, Part B, and supplemental health insurance. Without costs or fees to you, Medicaid pays all necessary medical bills. Contact the Social Security office in your area and get full information.

There are Community Health Services in many areas to help keep you healthy at the lowest possible costs. Phone City Hall to find out about these services in your community.

In addition, there may be a supportive services program in your area which provides home care for people of limited income. It may not be necessary for you to go to some institution. Again, contact City Offices and get any information about this program.

A person doesn't have to be a hypochondriac to take advantage of medical services that help him enjoy better health. But he must value himself, including his body, as a child of God!

Charles Victor de Bonstetten, the Swiss author, expressed

the purpose of this chapter when he wrote, "To resist the
frigidity of old age, one must combine the body, the mind,
and the heart. And to keep these in parallel vigor, one must
exercise, study, and love." [14]

5.

Me, Me, Me—
There's No One But Me!

*"No wise man ever wished
to be younger."*
—*Jonathan Swift*

In this chapter, I deal with the subject of companionship, which is another major need in retirement years. However, since the problems of older married couples are in many ways different from those of senior singles, my approach to companionship must be considered in two parts. The first section of this chapter is for older persons who are blessed with a living spouse; it contains fifteen ways to keep life in a long marriage by building reverence, love, and respect. The second section is for those who live alone—both those who have never married and those who find themselves suddenly single after the death of a husband or wife. The single life is one of the most serious problems in older years. I suggest six door-openers for finding the kind of companionship you need.

MARRIED OLDER PERSONS

I was asked to lead a forty-eight-hour marriage seminar. About one hundred couples attended, representing various church backgrounds—Baptists, Disciples of Christ, Episcopalians, Methodists, Nazarenes, Pentecostals, Presbyterians, and Roman Catholics. Their ages ranged from twenty-five to seventy, and the majority of them already had serious problems in their marriages. They were upstanding citizens; some were prominent leaders in their community. At the beginning of the seminar, I passed out a "Marriage Rating Questionnaire" which, among other things, required that they sum up their marriage as they saw it by checking one of several words listed. The word most commonly checked was "Blah." I interpret "Blah" to mean, "I need a meaningful relationship!"

Forget the idea that superiority of husband over wife or wife over husband is the issue. The central need is *relationship*. Reverence, love, and respect are the ingredients of the successful marriage relationship. This love is not only gushy sentiment or warm feelings—it also includes acts of a loving nature which sometimes may *not* be accompanied by that warm, scintillating emotion Americans customarily call "love." The following are builders of reverence, love, and respect.

1. Request Rather Than Demand

The iron-fisted boss in marriage, whether the person be male or female, never builds genuine relationship. To request rather than demand does.

In Shakespeare's *Taming Of The Shrew,* Petruchio managed to get the hand of Katherine in marriage. She was a wild one, yet they weren't a bad match for each other. Petruchio's one driving ambition was to tame his newly acquired wife, and he directed himself to the task. She resisted with all her might, but Petruchio was determined to succeed.

In the process of trying to tame Katherine, he left her out in the cold, out in the rain, and alone in an unsightly castle with its bats and bugs. He forced her to do menial labor. When Petruchio said that black was white and white was black, he wanted Katherine to meekly agree. When he said that the sun was shining at two o'clock in the morning, he wanted Katherine to reply, "Petruchio, my worthy husband, you're so right. It is the sun shining at two o'clock this morning." In a matter of time, he achieved his goal, as far as he could tell.

The big test came when Katherine's family gathered for a holiday feast. All the women were in one room while their husbands talked and drank in another room. One fellow suggested, "Let's see how obedient our wives are by sending a servant to each one with this message: 'Your husband *commands* you to come to him this moment.' " All voiced their agreement except Petruchio.

"Oh, come on," the men insisted, "be a good sport." When Petruchio finally consented, the room rocked with laughter because Katherine's independence was a household word. To make the game more interesting, some sizeable bets were placed on Katherine! The odds were that Katherine would laugh in Petruchio's face and scorn the messenger who conveyed the message.

The game began and all the women refused to heed the command of their husbands. Then Katherine's moment arrived. Half of England had been wagered on her response. Reluctantly, the messenger whispered, "Your husband *asks* you to come to his side." Before her rage could erupt, the servant quickly scampered out of the room. As the men anxiously waited, seconds seemed like minutes. Katherine did not appear, yet, it was strange that they had not heard any commotion from her chambers.

Then, the doors to the men's chamber burst open. In walked a calm and collected Katherine. To the surprise of everyone, she brought with her the other wives as she reprimanded them for disregarding their husbands.

The curtain closes as Petruchio embraces Katherine and together they walk away. Shakespeare considered Katherine a shrewd manipulator, for in taming Katherine, Petruchio was himself tamed.

As the years pass, couples tend to take one another for granted. They slip into the mistake of demanding and commanding a certain response.

"Ask" is a powerful three letter word which is vital to the

marriage relationship. Demands destroy, but requests rejoice! The attitude prevalent in asking rather than commanding revives, rebuilds, and enlarges the relationship.

2. Be Tolerant with One Another

A man and his wife came to seek my help. In exasperation, the husband said, "Twenty-five years we've been married and still my wife tries to correct every statement I make." She said, "It's been twenty-six years, dear." Tolerance makes room for a relationship to grow. Marriage is the basic institution where tolerance is a necessity, but how often are you more tolerant with neighbors and other friends than the one closest to you?

3. Be Honest with Each Other

Once in awhile, ministers are pleased with a particular sermon and think they have done a superb job in the pulpit. As we drove home after one such occasion, I said (rather modestly, I thought), "I wonder how many great preachers there are in the world?" and my wife answered, "Well, there's one less than you think there is."

For your sake, you need your spouse to be honest with you. For your spouse's sake, you need to be honest. However, a satisfying relationship is best served when honesty comes from a spirit of goodwill and not from spite, revenge, or an "I told you so" spirit.

4. Differ Without Being Difficult

An older couple said, "It's no use. Differences have destroyed our relationship." Yet I have known couples who were so much alike that they were miserable. Differences can be allowed to either demote and destroy or lift and liberate a relationship. To differ without being difficult, try the following suggestions:

1) *Think of your differences as an asset instead of a liability.* The Creator has chosen to make you different from each other; for example, in appearance. My wife should be thrilled that she doesn't have to look like me—six feet, six inches tall, large feet, prematurely grey (I don't use Grecian Formula 16!), a scar on my left index finger, a birthmark in the vicinity of my left armpit, and a pointed nose.

Not even identical twins are absolutely identical. Totalitarian states have tried for centuries to hammer differences into oneness and make a mass people, a mass-mind. They have yet to succeed, because God has deemed it best that we be individual persons. The glory of marriage is not that the husband and wife are of one mind in respect to every thought and issue, but that they maintain a basic unity in spite of varying thoughts and differences of opinion.

2) *Assure yourself that most differences are not as big as you think.* Human beings have a habit of blowing disagreements out of proportion.

3) *Consider the facts available to you.* Facts and rumors are usually miles apart.

4) *Quickly admit you are wrong when you see that you are wrong.* It takes a big person to admit when he is wrong. Any child can insist he is right when in his heart he knows better.

5) *Respect the other person's right to believe for himself and express himself.* You expect the same of the other person in regards to you.

6) *Look beyond what you think is error in the other person's thinking.* Look deep enough to get to the heart.

7) *Emphasize your agreements.* Arguments and contention result from an emphasis on disagreements. Have you ever seriously argued over an agreement? If you harp on disagreement and you magnify it, then the disagreement looms so large that it directs you into needless confrontation.

8) *Base your own discussion on an understanding which takes into account that you are human.* "As I see it . . ." "According to my understanding . . ." "From my experi-

ence . . ." are phrases you need to keep close to your conversations. Use them often.

5. Let Your Partner Be Himself or Herself

Do not expect husband and wife to be the echo of someone else. Dr. David Reuben, the well-known marriage counselor, quoted a young husband as saying, "I couldn't believe it. Just because I suggested that Janet take some cooking lessons, she dumped the dinner down the sink and locked herself in the bathroom. I mean, my mother never did that." [1]

In older years, too, your mate must be your mate and not some other person—not a father, or brother, or mother, or sister, or neighbor, or friend substitute. And by no means is your husband or wife to be a ditto of yourself! This means that the routine for the day which has developed over many years should not be expected to drastically and suddenly change. You will see what I mean in the case of a couple whom I shall refer to as Blanche and Henry.

Blanche said, "Since Henry retired, he thinks he has quickly become a culinary expert and housekeeping whiz. For over forty years, I cooked enjoyable, well-balanced meals. What makes him act as if I can't cook anymore? He's always meddling in the kitchen and giving out advice on how to clean the house and wash the clothes."

Henry said, "Now that I have more time at home, Blanche acts like I'm the world's best carpenter, an accomplished yardman, and experienced painter. She's always on me to fix this, that, and the other thing."

Retirement doesn't qualify your spouse to be anyone other than oneself! Let your Blanche continue as the cook and housekeeper without interference. Respond when she asks your help. Stay out from under her feet. It is a mistake to unload additional work and a new set of rules and expectations on her. Keep away from her coattail.

Allow your Henry to develop his own routine for retirement years. You probably thought with all the newly-found time, Henry would whip odds and ends into shape overnight. A sensible suggestion might work, but seldom will nagging accomplish anything more than an argument or a retreat into a shell.

6. Reinforce One Another in the Presence of Others

Never belittle your mate while others are around. Dr. Reuben states, "The one characteristic above all others that distinguishes marriages that last from those that don't is the willingness of husband and wife to testify in each other's behalf." [2]

This is demonstrated by a couple who stood in line to weigh their luggage before they boarded a flight to the Bahamas. Each passenger was asked to give his own weight. This couple was oddly matched. The man was short and slight whereas the wife was a towering, ample figure who looked to be twice the size of her husband. When they got to the front of the line, the husband whispered to the custom's clerk, "That will be a total of three hundred thirty-eight pounds for the Lawrences."

7. Involve Each Other in Family Finances— Spending, Giving, Planning

How often is it that the wife knows nothing about family money unless there is a shortage of it! Dr. Reuben refers in his article to the wife who said, "Doctor, the thing about being married that annoys me the most is having to ask Jim for housekeeping money. It's like being back with my father again. I even get this little-girl voice." [3]

Now, you are retired. A wonderful new life is open to you. In some manner, your mate has had a hand in getting where you are. In the older years, involvement in family finances is just as important a role for *both* persons as it should have been during the working years. Some hold to the selfish idea that finances come in a "his/her" package.

If either one has been left out of financial matters during

employment years, this certainly is the time to reverse the pattern. Furthermore, one of you will inevitably have to deal with the finances when the spouse passes away. It is an unnecessary shock to have that responsibility dumped on your mate suddenly and without preparation.

8. Share With Each Other the Activities of the Day and Hopes for the Future

One sure signal of a marriage in trouble is when couples think in terms of "I" instead of "we." A stubborn silence is substituted for healthy communication. I am reminded of the older couple who was told their problem was a lack of communication. The wife said to her husband, "Now that we've learned to communicate, shut up!"

Common-sense communication is a sharing in which the goal is not to think alike as much as it is to think *together*. Your lives are important to one another; therefore, you need to talk about events which transpire each day. Sharing hopes and dreams pull you into the future with a sense of aim, togetherness, and harmony.

9. Find Something Positive to Say

Positive words produce positive feelings and cheerful words construct a cheerful spirit in you and your spouse. They help set the spiritual and emotional tone to solve problems.

10. When Disagreements Come Up, Meet One Another at Least Halfway

There used to be a tribe in Africa which practiced this builder. When one of its members didn't get along with someone, no matter what the reason, he took the responsibility of restoring the relationship. He visited the medicine man and confessed his feelings. Then he got a little fruit known as rulani which means, "Let there be peace." After that, he went to the person with whom he had the difference and told the events which caused him to feel as he did. As he closed, he crushed the rulani and threw it to the winds, saying, "As I have destroyed and thrown away these useless bits, I also crush and discard the resentful feelings which I have against you. Now let us have peace."

It is not of supreme importance who takes the first step or who is right. The essential need is that the first step be taken to resolve the disagreement or accept it amicably and go on enjoying one another.

11. Surprise Each Other Occasionally With Something Special

A special surprise when there is no special occasion makes a person feel special. One of our basic needs is to feel significant and worthwhile. In marriage, it is the privilege and responsibility to contribute to the sense of significance in your partner.

After many years of marriage, a husband decided to do this. He thought that instead of grumbling something like, "When will supper be ready?" he would give his wife a bouquet of flowers and a box of chocolates. When he got home, he went to the front door instead of using the door from the garage. The man rang the doorbell. When his wife answered, he stood there smiling from ear to ear, holding out the flowers and box of candy. Unaccustomed to such treatment, she declared crankily, "Look, Fred, our granddaughter Tammy has the flu, the washing machine has broken down, and I blew a fuse today. Now, you make my day perfect by coming home drunk!"

12. Express Yourself Tactfully

You may wonder the reason for tact since you have been married for many years. "Can't we just let our hair down and forget this kind of stuff." Two incidents answer the question.

I watched a woman who appeared to be about seventy years of age as she rode the merry-go-round at Disney World.

At the end of the ride, an attendant said, "You look younger." She asked, "Younger than what?" He answered, "Younger than when you got on." She laughed and rode the horses again!

One evening my wife and I joined an older couple for dinner. As we ate a meal fit for a king, the man said, "This is to make up for my birthday which she forgot." His wife replied, "Well, honey, how could you expect me to remember when you don't look any older!" All of us got a big laugh and he beamed with pride.

You can put to use the good tool of tact or you can be as sharp as a tack. No one enjoys being around a tack, but a tactful person is fun to live with!

13. Don't Forget the Value of Sexual Activity

One of the most common assumptions is that age eliminates sexual activity. It is more taboo than truth. Dr. Matthew E. Fairbanks, to whom I have already referred, writes, "As we know, all physical reactions slow down in the aged. Men find they react in slow time and all too frequently accept the social belief that sex stops for the aged and avoid sexual contact." He said that many men and women in their eighties and nineties are active sexually.[4]

An older person said, "I got so cold last night that I couldn't sleep." A grandchild asked, "Did your teeth chatter?" "I don't know," the older person replied, "we didn't sleep together." Unfortunately, this is reality for many older couples.

Of course, some suffer physical handicaps which prevent sexual activity. But many more suffer emotional handicaps and use age or some physical explanation as an excuse for abstinence. "At our age?" "What would our friends think?" "Our children would laugh at us!" "That's for younger people!"

You remain a human being for as long as you have a body! As a human being, you and your marriage partner have needs which can be fulfilled when you express your love for each other by a sexual relationship. In the final analysis, you are responsible only to God, yourself, and one another!

14. Pray Together

I know a successful marriage counselor who advises, "Prayer seems naive to a lot of people these days, but it has always been one of my favorite prescriptions for an ailing marriage." Praying together magnetizes people together around divine love and power. A few moments a day is a beginning. Get started and it will get easier.

15. Worship Together

In one of her columns, Dr. Joyce Brothers, the celebrated counselor, deals with "Religious Attitudes." One of the true or false choices reads, "Religious views have little relation to marital happiness." Dr. Brothers answered, "False. Studies indicate that religious persons are more happy in their marriages." [5] The inner life, energy, and desire derived from worship make available the basis required for a solid relationship in marriage.

All of us are familiar with Benjamin Franklin. Perhaps the most popular conception of this great man in American history is the story of his holding a kite during a thunderstorm. A lad in Philadelphia was asked to write an essay on Mr. Franklin's life. Although his treatment of Mr. Franklin was not very scholarly, it was to the point:

Benjamin Franklin was born in Boston but he soon got tired of that and moved to Philadelphia. When he got to Philadelphia he was hungry so he bought a loaf of bread. He put the bread under his arm. He walked up the street. He passed a woman. The woman smiled at him. He married the woman and discovered electricity.

By whose standard is your marriage relationship in older years to be void of "electricity?" You have a God-granted right for the relationship to grow and become more meaningful than you have ever experienced. Don't let taboos about age, pressures, and opinions deny the enjoyment available to you!

SINGLE SENIORS

At the beginning of this chapter, I said that the single life is one of the most serious problems in older years. Among the most cherished human relationships are love and friendship, but family and friends pass away. It is common for a retired person to lament, "Me, me, me—there's no one but me!"

Sixty percent of those sixty-five years and older live alone, as compared to a twenty percent average for those under sixty-five. More effort has been put into helping people reach retirement years than into helping them enjoy those years. Especially is this noticeable among older persons who face all or part of retirement life alone. In exasperation, a woman insisted, "Mr. Ray, tell the husbands to train their wives to be widows!"

Many of the older persons who live alone are women, because wives tend to live longer than their spouses. There is no use claiming that wives drive husbands to an early grave! Probably the reasons women enjoy a longer life-span include greater respect for their bodies (evidenced by more regular visits to the doctor), and more adequate handling of emotions. But whether the surviving partner is a woman or a man, the experience of being left alone can be traumatic.

For most people, the death of a spouse is life's most upsetting experience. This response is completely natural because the human relationship of a lifetime comes to an end. Very few people, even those whose marriage relationship has been volatile, agree with the following epitaph:

> Here lies my wife,
> Here let her lie,
> Now she's at rest
> And so am I.[6]

This loss can become either a door to a new life or a defeat which paralyzes life. A friend said, "Virginia is gone. What is there for me to live for?" Despite repeated encouragement from children, neighbors, and church, he gave up emotionally and spiritually. Four years later, a funeral was held for him, but in his heart he had died within three months of his wife's death. This response is unnatural and unnecessary.

How can the loss of a companion become a door to life? That depends on the use of some of the following door openers in the months and years following the funeral service. Older persons who have never married but have lost friends and job contacts can make use of the same suggestions.

1. Don't Frown on "Sunset Marriages." They're Okay!

I heard about a husband who was so devoted to his wife that when she died he had printed on her tombstone, "The light of my life has gone out." About six months later, he met another woman who won his affection. They married. After the ceremony, someone wrote on his first wife's tombstone, "But he struck another match." [7]

There is an old notion that second marriages which come late in life are usually disastrous. The claim is that an older person is so cemented to memories of the former spouse that another relationship is impossible. You may have been told that, as you grow older, you become so set in your ways that you are unable to adapt to someone else. Possibly you have understood that a "sunset" marriage serves only the purposes of convenience and companionship and that sexual involvement is out of the question.

In fact, older persons are inclined to bring more tolerance to new marriages than younger people; therefore, the degree of success in these marriages has been found to be appreciably higher than the national average! After all, the older person has many years of valuable experience behind him.

Furthermore, the flexibility demonstrated in late-life marriages is often greater than in younger couples! It is true that memories of a deceased spouse tend to be more present in the mind of the surviving mate than those of any other person, including those who are living. However, over a period of time, the dominance of these memories can be transferred to someone else. And it is okay if they are!

Convenience and companionship are important factors in "sunset" marriages, but do not discount the possibility of sexual involvement. Sexual enjoyment does not have an arbitrary age limit to it!

An older person agreed on every point I have written, then asked, "How do I find a possibility without being pushy?"

1) You can begin by *being yourself*. A false face does not deeply win a person or build a meaningful relationship in the event one starts.

2) *Improve yourself.* No one is as good and great as he can become. A man said, "I'm not as good as I ought to be, but I'm not as bad as I could be." It is *not* too late to change! As you improve, you will become more fun to other people and yourself.

3) *Become the "right" person.* In marriage, many people want to find the perfect partner. This is a case of imperfection seeking perfection when the need is not so much in finding the "right" person as in becoming the "right" person.

4) *Involve yourself in group activities.* Exposure is important, but the activities need to have value to you and others. I met my wife in church when I was not particularly looking for a person to marry. There are civic, community, and neighborhood projects. Various social events and clubs are open to you. Since it is to your advantage to avoid the reputation of being an older person on the prowl for a husband or wife, select activities which meet the standard of value for purposes other than getting a spouse. This indirect method is more workable.

5) *Trust your need to God.* You don't have to fret and worry. He is wise and your best interests are very crucial to him. As Dr. Charles H. Spurgeon, the English minister, said, "You may not always trace God's hand, but you can always trust His heart." [8]

6) *Take as much time as you need.* Sometimes you may

feel like the parishioner who said, "Lord, I need patience and I need it *now!*" Maybe the blessing of a late-life marriage will come your way, but you don't have to rush yourself or someone else. Often a rush brings disappointment.

2. Develop a Buddy Plan

Everyone needs at least one other person who can check on him each day. In turn, each one needs someone on whom he can check. A telephone call is sufficient. At times you may want to visit one another, shop together, and attend various church, community, and social gatherings with each other. This is level-headed action to overcome the serious problem of isolation. But to develop a buddy plan, there are some rules to observe. They are contained in a senior citizen's prayer which was given to me.

Lord, Thou knowest better than I know myself that I am growing older.
Keep me from getting too talkative, and thinking
　　I must say something on every subject and on every occasion.
Release me from craving to straighten out everybody's affairs.
Teach me the glorious lesson that occasionally it is possible that
　　I may be mistaken.
Make me thoughtful, but not moody; helpful, but not bossy.
　　Thou knowest, Lord, that what I want most is a few friends
　　at the end.

3. Avoid Being an "A-giner"

An attorney invited Clarence Darrow, the famous criminal lawyer and a dissenter most of his life, to participate in a debate. When asked if he were familiar with the subject, Mr. Darrow answered, "No." The other man queried, "Then how can you engage in a debate?" "It's easy," Mr. Darrow stated. "I'll take the negative side. I can argue *against* anything!" [9]

An "a-giner" is a nuisance to himself and others. People shy away from negative people. As a single person, you need people and they need you, but they will not take you at the expense of their own frame of mind.

Do you tend to see what is wrong with someone or something before you see what is right? Is your first response usually a "can't," "won't," or "don't"? You might think, "But I'm right some of the time." Does that compensate for the many times the "a-gining" position is wrong? After all, a clock which has quit running is accurate twice each day, but what about the rest of the time?

You can overcome this problem. My Grandfather Ray was an "a-giner" who had undisputed claim as a top-rated grouch. While in town one Saturday, a shoeshine boy asked, "Shine, mister?" Granddad growled, "Nope." The boy replied, "I'll shine 'em so you can see your face in 'em." Granddad retorted, "I said, 'No!'" The boy saw how sour he looked and mumbled, "Mister, I don't blame you. I wouldn't want to see a face like that either."

Although Granddad was a good man—hard-working, honest, loyal—his disposition had a destructive effect on his life until he began to change for the better. This change started at Granny's death, when Granddad was almost eighty!

4. Expect Good to Happen to You

Thomas Carlyle, the noted Scottish philosopher, claimed that the Age of Miracles is forever here and that those who *expect* a miracle are the ones who most often experience one.[10] *The spirit of expectation conditions your life to realize the object of your expectation.* This spirit actualizes itself in experience, depending on the intensity of that expectation. It is the spiritual foundation from which the real stuff comes. The seeds of expectation implant themselves in your thoughts, ingrain themselves in your desires, fire up motivation, and work themselves out through action. As a result, they affect your personality, habits of life—indeed, everything about you.

During a conversation with an older couple whose family had a serious problem, a woman lamented, "I don't expect any miracles!" I interrupted her to say, "Please do!" Rather dumbfounded, she asked, "Please do what?" I replied, "Please do expect a miracle!"

According to a report in *Family Magazine,* as long as you *expect* to be "unlucky," you will generally *be* "unlucky." (I use the word "luck" only because the article used it. I, personally, don't put much stock in "luck." I prefer providence and pluck!) "A person's [expectation] . . . determines to a very large extent the degree to which his efforts are crowned with luck or good fortune." [11] It is like the man who prays for rain, then carries an umbrella to work with him! Do you expect a miracle or a mistake? A star or a scar?

5. Accept and Apply Love Where You Are

Hate and ill-will clog up the pipe through which life and relationships flow. Football fans remember Vince Lombardi who coached the Green Bay Packers when they were nearly invincible. After the team's Super Bowl victory, he was asked to explain their success. Mr. Lombardi answered, "They won because they love each other. You know what kind of love I mean. It's the kind that means loyalty, teamwork, respecting the dignity of another, willingness to make sacrifices—heart power, not hate power. This is the love the Packers have for each other." [12]

What an explanation for a football team! It certainly is true of life. You can better handle life as a single person when you accept love from others and apply love where you are, as you are, by what you say and do. Do not make the mistake of thinking you must have a feeling of love before you speak or act out love. You can act in a manner of goodwill whether or not you possess a feeling of goodwill.

6. Be the Kind of Person People Want As a Friend

As a general rule, people respond in a manner similar to what they see in those to whom they respond. I think of it as the "similar to" and "extension of" principle. It means that kind most often attracts the same kind. As a result, a person picks out strengths and weaknesses in others which correspond to his or her own strengths and weaknesses.

Dr. James A. Hadfield alluded to this remarkable truth when he wrote, "Repressed complexes which we refuse to recognize tend to attach themselves to persons and objects of the outside world. Thus, we condemn in others what we refuse to admit in ourselves. This is the principle of the objectification or projection of our complexes. The principle may be stated thus: 'Our relation to the outside world is determined by our relation to our complexes.' " [13]

To put it plainly, if your friends are complainers, you should consider the possibility that you are an overly-critical person. If they are happy, probably you are a happy person.

Are you an inspiring person? Do you stimulate cheerfulness in others? Are you a friendly, sensible, sensitive individual? Do you express genuine concern for others? Can you be trusted? Is life a joyful journey for you? Do you have sympathy and empathy for people when they hurt? Do you respect people for who they are—persons—more than for what they possess? Are you congenial? Do you express appreciation to others?

Life as a senior single is meant to be *life*. It begins with the spirit reflected in these lines:

> This also, that I live,
> I consider a gift of God. [14]

6.

End Your Search For Self-Worth

*"Life does not count by years.
Some suffer a lifetime in a day,
and so grow old between the
rising and setting of the sun."*
—*Augusta Jane Evans*

I asked a man in his seventies how he would like living to be one hundred. "No," he responded, "God, no!" Why this answer? "Because I'm nothing since I retired. It is unbearable to think this would go on another twenty-six years!" The gentleman demonstrated one of the basic losses many older people suffer—a loss of dignity.

I consider a loss of dignity to be the loss of the sense of personal worth. Dr. Carl J. Jung, the famous European psychologist, succinctly outlined the problem:

We all say that this is the century of the common man, that he is the lord of the earth, the air and the water, and that on his decision hangs the historical fate of the nations. This proud picture of human grandeur is unfortunately an illusion only and is counterbalanced by a reality which is very different. In this reality man is the slave and victim of the machines that have conquered space and time for him; he is intimidated and endangered by the might of the war technique which is supposed to safeguard his physical existence; his spiritual and moral freedom, though guaranteed within limits in one half of his world, is threatened with chaotic disorientation, and in the other half it is abolished altogether. Finally, to add comedy to tragedy, this lord of the elements, this universal arbiter,

81

hugs to his bosom notions which stamp his dignity as worthless and turn his autonomy into an absurdity." [1]

WHAT CAUSES THE LOSS?

The source of this loss of individual dignity can be found in the individual himself, his circumstances, in business, government and society.

1. Radical Dependence on Vocation

Too often, people depend on their job to give them identification, fulfilment, and direction as persons. This is one of the ingredients in the formula for personal worth, but a problem occurs when the job becomes the only source. I remember the woman who said, "If it weren't for my job, I wouldn't have any reason to live."

A person may become overabsorbed with the career from which livelihood is drawn. Then, when vocational life ends— retirement—the person begins a gradual decline as the feeling of nothingness creeps over him.

2. Death of a Spouse

I believe that a little bit of us dies when a loved one passes away. The hurt inside is almost indescribable when the person was close to us. One with whom many years may have been invested is no longer a companion, confidant, lover, helper, encourager, and supporter.

Grief is a normal expression of emotions; however, utter remorse is defeating because it debilitates a sense of personal worth when it is clung to over a long period of time.

3. Compulsory Retirement

Earlier retirement is a reality in western civilization. In the armed forces, some complete their twenty years while they are in their thirties; other wind up thirty years when they are under fifty. In government and industry, many people are retiring in their fifties and early sixties. Some retirees choose to move from a vocational to a more leisurely life. Others are forced!

To a significant number of older persons—those who have chosen to retire as well as those who had no option—retirement has led to a degenerating feeling of little or no worth. The biggest problem, however, is for those who fell victim to an inflexible, arbitrary retirement policy.

I know many people in this group. A man of enormous abilities, drive, and energy was put aside because "it's company rules." This insensitive removal from a high and responsible office has hurt him deeply. Now, five years after his retirement, he is still struggling with feelings of being no longer needed, of being put aside. And he could probably perform as commendably in his job now as he did twenty years ago. The experience of my friend is repeated thousands of times daily in industry, government, and institutions throughout the United States.

4. Treatment As a "Has-Been"

This is a tragic development for a person and it initiates a traumatic loss of a sense of personal worth. "I'm over the hill . . . on the shelf . . . to the sidelines." Feeling cast off by business and society, a person wastes potential and deprecates the experience and wisdom with which the years have blessed him. "I'm second-class now," he thinks.

I once met a woman who for thirty years had been executive secretary to a prominent official in a national company. The intricacies of her job had exposed her to all facets of the industry. Probably she had become as qualified as her boss to hold a vice president's job.

Abrupt retirement (company policy, naturally!) brought on the vicious has-been syndrome. When she joined my church, I was impressed with her capabilities, so I approached her about one of my projects which needed a top-notch office coordinator. It required expertise and command of time and direction of schedules. The "has-been" mentality had so infiltrated her personality that it took a while to persuade her that she could do the job. But once she did, the woman became a marvelous and most efficient coordinator. Later she confessed, "This has made me a new person. I'm not a 'has-been' after all!"

5. A Bombardment Of "Helplessness"

The prevailing attitude of government and, to some degree, society, is that the retired person is helpless. As a result, he is bombarded by "we'll do it *for* you."

Yes, some older persons are totally helpless. Physical condition, inflation on a meager and fixed income, and other circumstances have stripped them of the ability to care for themselves in the manner they need and deserve. *It is our responsibility to care for them*—family, church, friends, and government.

But for the majority of older persons, such an approach is ridiculous. Sadly, not everyone can dispel the helplessness bombardment. Confronted with the news that "you are no longer able to manage for yourself, so we'll do it for you," often enough, long enough, people begin to accept it as truth. Although intentions are good, the price it exacts on a sense of personal worth is high.

INDICATIONS OF A LOSS OF THE SENSE OF PERSONAL WORTH

There are five tell-tale indications of the person who loses his sense of personal worth.

1. Boredom

One of the surest indicators is boredom—the awful illness and paralysis of older age. Challenges will help people keep boredom out of their lives or, at least, at a diminished level. But the great challenge to live meaningfully in older years is unaccepted by many retired persons. There is a floating restlessness when honest-to-goodness self-esteem is trampled. A sixty-seven-year-old demonstrated it when he said, "I don't think much of myself. Give me a good reason as to why I should! I don't think much of life either."

In an attempt to cope with boredom, unnecessary drugs are sometimes used to the extent that they become an escape mechanism. Oh, in most cases the medication is prescribed as treatment for some physical malady. But the root sickness is boredom. If it were cured, the physical sickness would also find its cure.

2. Depression

Another indicator is depression. This disease of the spirit kills more older persons than cancer, strokes, and pneumonia. The individual is dulled to the opportunities offered by life each day. Depression drains away motivation and desire. Unable to make up his mind, the depressed person is suspended in a state of indecisiveness and aimlessness. He notices a nagging tiredness; complaints increase; interest in others subsides; self-criticism becomes commonplace; and he may suffer from insomnia.

I have a close friend who used to awake at all hours of the night with a gnawing, agonizing feeling in the pit of his stomach. The worst of thoughts crowded his mind. Then he began to blame God for the plight in which he found himself. "Well, you wouldn't believe it!" he explained. "I went to church last Sunday and I declare, all these bad things which have happened to me this week! I'm not going again anytime soon!"

3. Unmanageable Problems

The older person who loses his sense of personal worth usually becomes problem-oriented. He thinks problems; consequently, they are magnified out of proportion. The result is that he considers them unmanageable.

A retired woman moaned, "My aches and pains—no one suffers like I do. There's no way I can cope with my situation. No one deserves the condition I'm in." When a person thinks this way, the power to cope with problems ebbs and the person becomes victimized by them.

4. Isolation

A combination of boredom, depression, and the feeling that problems are unmanageable causes isolation. "Oh, leave me alone." "I don't want to do anything, see anybody, go anywhere."

This withdrawal into a shell limits conversation and contact with others. The person is apt to become a loner, even though he might have been an outgoing, congenial individual in years past. At this extreme, personality is altered in the wrong direction.

5. Death-Wish

These forces gang-up on the older person and give birth to a death-wish. "I wish I'd go ahead and die." "There's nothing to keep me here." "I'd be better off dead." "Others would be better off if I'd go ahead and die." An older person once told me, "It's always easier to go to heaven than face the challenge of living in a world like mine."

Some older persons go as far as to take their own lives. But a larger number simply possesses the death-wish secretly. They would never kill themselves with pills, a gun, poison, or a deliberate automobile wreck. Nevertheless, they wouldn't mind if an accident or a coronary happened suddenly. The death-wish is most apt to occur after the death of a marriage mate.

WHAT CAN BE DONE ON A SOCIETAL LEVEL?

Part of the answer to conditions I have discussed is on the hands of society as a whole. In the Western nations, especially the United States, industrialization and mobility have profoundly affected the way of life. This has resulted in some good, such as a better quality of life, higher incomes, more leisure time, and greater access to travel.

On the other hand, our response to industrialization and mobility has contributed to a de-emphasis on the aged. The most obvious sign of this decline is the relaxation in family unity. Brothers, sisters, and children assume less responsibility for older members of the family. In many instances, hundreds of miles separate members of families, whereas in past generations whole families clustered in the same community, rarely moving more than a few miles from one another. The old idea of "out of sight, out of mind" is often the case.

Society needs a radical change in its concept of the retired person! Some answers must be found and utilized, especially since scientists around the world are now developing the know-how to delay the aging process for many years. With the circumstances which are increasingly prevalent in modern society, what can be done on a societal level?

1. Accept Older Persons

Society's new concept of those growing older can begin with an acceptance of the retired as persons. To me, this means that older persons are a part of the mainstream. They are *not* adopted children, illegitimate offspring, fifth wheels, hangers-on, or spare tires—at best only to be tolerated! They must be accepted as necessary and vital organs of a complete body-society. Individualized, the body has a head, arms, fingers, legs, feet, and toes. Accordingly, society has various ages—infants, children, young people, middle-agers, and older persons. Chop off a chunk of a body and that body cannot function.

Older people form an important segment of society. They come within the circle, too. Therefore, they need to be treasured, respected, and treated with acceptance.

2. Love

Closely aligned with acceptance of those growing older is love. This is a sincere appreciation which is shown in our relationships with older persons. The word that stands out most in my mind is *personalization*.

Older people have suffered the most from a depersonalized society. More than any other segment of the populace, the retired community feels the sharp pain of "they don't really care about me anymore." Computerized and highly-mobile societies have suffered enormously from this depreciation of the person. Dr. Paul Tournier has pointed out that when there is a negative balance between the wealth of technological emphasis (which is value determined by one's ability to produce) and personal relationships fostered by love, we tend to underscore technological wealth.[2] For a long time, the gap between technology and personal relationships has grown and relationships have borne the awful consequences. Overmechanization has occurred at the expense of love.

But it does not have to be that way. Business can begin to recognize its responsibility to the *whole* person rather than production capacity only. This love of which I write is the impetus essential to moving from a "thing" society to a "person" society. As Dr. Tournier states, "Love requires a commitment."[3]

It is now time for industry to admit that the complete person is more than an ability to manipulate nuts and bolts, and that when the whole person is recognized, his ability increases and his motivation and performance improve! Any store with an operation larger than the mom-and-pop variety can begin to provide opportunity for employees to enlarge their horizons. Business can start to help employees prepare emotionally, mentally, and physically—as well as financially—for retirement. Industry can begin to maintain contact with employees who have retired.

I am aware of a great department store chain in the South which follows its retired employees until they die. They are remembered at birthdays and Christmas. Under no compulsion other than love, the president sees to it that the income of employees who have given many years of faithful service is augmented by a monthly check from the company comptroller.

Management might charge that this practice reduces that little god called "profit." Naturally, it requires some expense. But you should witness the diligence, attitude, and production of active workers, not to mention the goodwill of those who have retired! Furthermore, employee turnover is half what it is in competing stores! The president claimed, "It doesn't cost the company a penny in the final analysis."

3. Discard Discrimination

In my opinion, the presence of discrimination based on age is undeniable. Some companies flinch at hiring anyone over forty. People fifty-five years of age and older find it incredibly difficult to relocate professionally. Often, age makes the difference when it comes to a promotion: "Charlie has got the know-how and experience, but he's sixty!" Such discrimination is modern evidence that we despise growing older.

A letter to Dr. Joyce Brothers discusses the point:

I'm a man in my seventies and am amazed that while people now recognize bias against blacks, Jews and women as wrong, they seem unable to see the prejudice toward older Americans. Preconceived ideas of how an older person looks, thinks and feels are every bit as ridiculous as bias based on race, religion or gender. A liberated woman who would be furious with a man who told her her place was in the kitchen wouldn't hesitate to insult an older person. How do we overcome this kind of thinking? I'm a victim and I hate it.

The counselor replied:

Don't be passive and don't hesitate to point out to people that they are being bigoted and biased. I agree; people who are extremely sensitive to sexism and racism seem oblivious to bias toward age. Don't allow yourself to be victimized. Speak up just as you have in your letter. This doesn't mean you have to start a fight. You can make your views heard and felt if you're direct and polite.

When you see anything on television that is offensive to older people or that generalizes or reflects old stereotypes, sit down and write to the station and the sponsors. Believe me, this kind of protest has an impact. . . . Try to stimulate others in your community to fight prejudice too. Join as many senior citizens' groups as you can and encourage members to be vocal on this issue and not become lost as silent seniors. Older people could have a great deal of . . . clout if they organized, for they compose a formidable number . . . not easily ignored." [4]

Government, too, can become a force to get rid of discriminatory practices based on age! Your representatives and senators will hear you when you speak loudly enough!

4. Change from Compulsory Retirement to Voluntary-Individualized-Compulsory Retirement

We are told that thirty percent of retirees in a European country are retired against their wishes and that nearly seventy-three percent of the men and sixty-eight percent of the women, age sixty-six to seventy-two, want to continue on the job.[5] These figures could also apply to the United States.

Compulsory retirement at any age is a huge waste of potential. Arbitrarily, employees are terminated after twenty, twenty-five, or thirty years—or at age sixty, sixty-two, sixty-five, or sixty-eight. What is the rationale? Some answers which have come to me include:

We've got to make room for younger men.

The only way to get them out is force them out.

He couldn't do the job any longer.

It's a fact of company life.

We don't like our people dying on the job.

We feel our people ought to enjoy their last years.

At their age, they won't adapt to changing methods and new ideas.

One or two of the explanations make sense, but a policy for retirement could be most effective if it were flexible.

Dr. Arthur S. Flemming, the U.S. Commissioner on Aging, charged that compulsory retirement is a lazy man's device in direct conflict with the Judeo-Christian concept of the dignity and worth of an individual. Speaking to several hundred business leaders at a symposium, he said, "Forced retirement and the unwillingness to hire older people is a deep-seated prejudice, namely agism." He also stated, "The lack of willingness to involve older persons in society is depriving us of services desperately needed." [6]

Older people who want to retire should be allowed to do so. Those who want to continue their employment years need to be considered on an individualized basis. Their attitude, ability, congeniality, professional know-how, energy, willingness to change, and physical condition must be taken into account. If the evidence is in favor of their continuation, they should remain employed. Those who want to continue working but do not qualify must be compelled to retire.

In most cases, retirement policy has been based on chronological age. *The system needs to be shifted from chronology to contribution!*

5. Listen To Older Persons

I talked with a very capable woman who had been retired for three years. She lived in an apartment complex with a large number of older persons. "There is more complaining than what is necessary," she commented, "but when you get below the surface, many of my neighbors really have something to say."

All too often, however, the end of employment years has been the end of listening years. Someone summarized it when he said, "Well, they've had their day." Productivity, in the sense of vocation, has ended for them. The weakness in society is the attitude that retirement age also brings an end to the ability to contribute ideas worthy of consideration.

We need to listen to the retired person—first, because older people are *persons* and all persons need someone to listen, and second, because many of them have something to say which is worthwhile! Their experience, knowledge, and perspective endow them with a very impressive inventory of qualifications. The rest of society can benefit from the retired community. Ideas submitted by older persons can produce some positive and helpful results for retirees and people of all ages.

6. Emphasize "With, By, and For"

It is a social tragedy to treat older persons as helpless, senility-ridden people when many of them are capable of doing more than even they think.

By doing for someone that which the individual can do for himself, we minimize the blessing of personal initiative and effort and glorify a dependency which shackles personality, dissipates drive, encourages laziness, and shortens life!

The well-being of society and the individual would be much better served if the emphasis were "with, by, and for" older people. They should be involved in a cooperative way—stimulated, challenged, and enabled to carry out programs and projects for themselves. Younger people should do for them no more than what they are unable to do for themselves. I believe this approach is valid all the way from government to the church and local club.

Several hundred older people in a congregation had become accustomed to the governing board making decisions on programs and projects which affected them as a group and executing those decisions. Then someone emphasized, "Why don't we suggest the basic ideas and let the older people decide, plan, and get the job done?" "Oh, that won't work," another member remarked. "We need to do it like we've always done. Besides, they deserve to take things easy." A third member responded, "Maybe *they* don't need us to do things like *we've* always done. Perhaps *they* deserve the chance to do it themselves."

This positive view prevailed and the results were splendid. The older people involved themselves in planning and execution of the program in a way that startled themselves and the congregation! The man who had taken a negative approach in the board meeting admitted, "I didn't think they had it in them!" It was a new birth in the life of those older people and a new day in programs directed toward their well-being.

WHAT YOU CAN DO FOR YOURSELF

After discussing what society can do to promote a sense of personal worth in the older person, I must outline some ideas which show what you can do for yourself. Understand that not every older person is at the total mercy of society and government! Very few members of the group as a whole are breathing vegetables—physically or emotionally!

1. Say Yes to Life

In my contacts with older persons, I have often heard this statement: "I've done my part. It's time for younger people to do theirs." To approach retirement years with a passive and resigned response is both uncalled for and unnecessary. *Claim life by accepting it with a resounding yes!*

Theodore Roosevelt stated, "The poorest way to face life is to face it with a sneer." [7] You may feel that in retirement life has dealt you a double hand, that it has played jokes on you and that you have been tricked. But despite the horrors from society's treatment of the older person and the spiritual barbarism which causes grief and appalls you, life now has the potential of great richness, joy, and adventure. Live as much as you can each day. Accept infirmities, afflictions, and unfulfilled dreams.

2. Live Your Age

rom one stage in
ness to move up
a more pathetic
ager. Why should
d when you *are*

sixty-five! Attempts to live younger betrays a ridiculous fear and resentment of growing older.

I know a man who made a fool of himself trying to be thirty when he was seventy. Inordinate attempts were made to cover the appearance of aging. Eventually, his health caved in because he made every effort to maintain the schedule of a young man. Family and friends were not wrong when they called him a "phony." In the end, this denial of age caught up with him.

There is a certain grace to getting older. The experience can include beauty, and power, and excitement! Living your age is the most wonderful mark of your age.

3. Make Yourself Useful Now

Surprisingly, more people than not are still working at age sixty-five. This is true at seventy. Almost half of the men are working at age seventy-five! Their secret is to make themselves useful now.

In his speech, Dr. Flemming underscored the point that "studies have shown non-involvement at any age causes rapid mental and physical deterioration."[8] Kyle Samuel Crichton, the American author, worded it nicely:

Life's a pretty precious and wonderful thing. You can't sit down and let it lap around you. . . . You have to plunge into it; you have to dive through it! And you can't save it, you can't store it up; you can't horde it in a vault. You've got to taste it; you've got to use it. The more you use, the more you have . . . that's the miracle of it![9]

Yet you do not have to be employed to make yourself useful. There are always projects around the house to which you can give yourself. What about your family and friends? The grandchildren are a wonderful investment of time and energy. Church, civic, and club enterprises need your help. Then there are neighbors for whom you can do things without being nosy. Life offers enough time and opportunity for you to make yourself useful *now*.

4. Keep Your Mind on the Grow

Every person needs to be forever learning. When he was past ninety, the famous cellist Pablo Casals was asked why he still practiced five to six hours each day. He replied, "Because I think I am improving." Justice Oliver Wendell Holmes was ninety-two when President Roosevelt asked him the reason he was reading Plato. The jurist answered, "Mr. President, to improve my mind." James Madison, the American president, stated, "Knowledge will forever govern ignorance and the people who mean to be their own governors must take care to arm themselves with the power that knowledge gives." [10]

Compare life to learning to play a musical instrument. You may master the techniques, but you must increase your knowledge of the instrument as you go along. What really makes the difference is what you learn after you know it all. To avoid a hardening of the mind, you need to keep it growing.

You can develop new skills and increase your knowledge by reading and attending the theater and concerts. One of the beautiful sights for me is to see an older person enrolled in college courses just for the sake of expanding his horizon.

In retirement, some enterprising people have developed new skills. A stock broker became an expert carpenter. A secretary qualified as a court reporter. A woman got her Master's Degree. A mechanic became an expert TV repairman. None of these friends involved themselves professionally in these pursuits; they used them around the house and neighborhood. What stimulated them? A desire to keep their mind on the grow.

5. Enjoy New Experiences

Each day is an opportunity to experience something new.
_____ experiences, one's spirit becomes stale

routine whenever possible. In this way, you expose yourself to new experiences.

A woman whose husband died said that for a long time she felt life wasn't worth living. "Then I thought, 'Well, Peg, you've got to pull out of this!' I decided to do something every day to make someone else happy." It was the first time in her life that she consciously, deliberately decided to do something each day to help another person to be happy. It was a new decision which started her on a journey of new experiences.

I asked, "What happened?" She responded, "I've found something more to my life. But just as important, I have enjoyed some wonderful new experiences." The woman explained that those new experiences have come from what she has done for others and from the people for whom she did them. Rather excitedly, she shared, "There are as many experiences as there are people."

6. Think of Yourself as God's Somebody

Anyone who has lost the sense of personal worth is likely to have a small concept of God or a concept of a small God. The result is that he thinks small about himself as a creation of God and his life as a gift from God.

Yet the fact remains—you are somebody by virtue of God's handiwork. No one else nor anything else was big and great enough to put you together. Thousands of years ago, a man possessed enough insight to write,

> [You] have been borne by me from your birth, carried from the womb; even to your old age I am He, and to gray hairs I will carry you. I have made, and I will bear; I will carry and will save (Isa. 4–6:34, RSV).

Increasing the sense of personal worth is like a solo flight, in that there is much you can do for yourself. A friend reminisced about the time he worried himself with attempts to change those around him. Employees and family members were cool toward his noble efforts. He said, "I decided I wasn't called to change *them*. I was called to change *me*." Besides, as parents painfully discover, human nature responds to what is seen in others. When they change their own behavior, Mom and Dad often find that their children are more apt to change.

You can be a part of the catalyst to change society's approach to older people. You can experience more immediate results in yourself when you do what is within your power to upgrade your own sense of personal worth.

7.

Your Life—
A Donation or Demand?

*"To me, old age is always
fifteen years older than I am."*
—*Bernard M. Baruch*

Now we consider at length the question of integration into society—which means simply being a part of the life of the community and nation. The problem of disintegration from society is real, even acute, to many older people. Business, government, community, and sometimes even the church isolate people into age groupings. Contact is confined to those of the same age. This separation is often followed by a response of withdrawal on the part of older persons.

One example of this is Mark, who retired from his job as an accountant with a large firm. At the office, he had intermingled with workers who ranged from thirty to sixty-five years old. Now, he was no longer "one of the boys." Retirement had suddenly sent him over the hill. Newly-found leisure time excited Mark for six months; then he began to feel the separation from associates, vocational activity, schedule, and the office, which had been a symbol of usefulness. He responded to the feeling of isolation by retreating into a shell. His life became a demand instead of a donation.

I believe that retirement centers, clubs and classes, and planned activities only for older people, as well-meaning as they are, can become forms of isolation from the mainstream of society, and therefore detrimental.

So that I will not be misunderstood, let me emphasize that

there is value in being with one's own group. Age produces similar interests and needs. The climate in the sunbelt of the United States is very attractive to those who have lived in sections of the country where there are harsh winters. Retiring in an area where the weather is less severe has advantages which cannot be disputed. Clubs, classes, and planned activities involving older persons are very helpful and, in my judgment, necessary.

However, for a person to direct his involvement, living, and association exclusively to those his own age indicates withdrawal and a disintegration from society! There are ways to counteract withdrawal and accomplish a more gratifying integration into society.

PARTICIPATE IN PROCESSES OF GOVERNMENT

One way to work toward integration into society is to participate in the processes of government. *The simplest method available is to cast your vote in local, state, and national elections.*

I have met older people who are disillusioned with government; they say things like, "My vote doesn't make any difference." "Who cares whether I vote?" "It doesn't matter who is elected. Things don't seem to improve." But there are many reasons your ballot is important.

In the first place, your vote stimulates a sense of personal pride. A man said, "I feel good when I vote. It makes me feel I'm a part of things." The vote also shows gratitude for the precious freedom to vote. The same man stated, "When I vote, I know I've done something which is denied to the majority of people on this earth. In a sense, the ballot box makes me a V.I.P.—a member of a select group."

Your vote is important to the enjoyment of better government. As a political science major in college, I came to the conclusion that government is no better than what the people at the grassroots insist it be. Government will be no worse than those same people allow it to be. In a democracy, it is still Mr. and Mrs. Everyday Citizen who ultimately make the difference. Neither democracy nor better government is dead unless the people upon whom it depends are dead. Woodrow Wilson wrote, "Liberty has never come from the government. Liberty has always come from the subjects of it." [1] So, review the issues in an election. Advocate policies that are wholesome and needed. Admonish political leaders when they seem to err.

Your vote also helps keep you functional. It is a noble action which expresses a consciousness of the society in which you live and of which you are a part. Point out a person who has withdrawn from life and I believe I can point out the same person who has lost the consciousness of society. Instead of thinking "we" and "us," he thinks "I" and "me."

I say it again: *vote!* When you are unable to go to the polls, arrange for the polls to come to you. Use an absentee ballot.

Another way to participate in the processes of government is to *get active in the machinery from which government is usually derived—precinct, county, state, and even national party organizations.* M. J. Brown, one of my parishoners, still serves on the City Zoning Board although he is retired. And he makes an effective contribution to the work of that group.

If government needs improving, you can help improve it by activity in caucuses and conventions. A United States representative told me that with three hundred committed workers, a person can win a congressional election in any district in the nation. He did it in a metropolitan area of five hundred thousand people.

Don't think that your involvement in the machinery of government has to absorb all your time and energy. It can be a part of your life—a piece of the pie and not the entire pie.

In addition to donating your time, *you can exercise the power of influence.* This is an essential ingredient in the processes of government. In an amicable way, seek to influence your councilman, commissioner, mayor, state senator and representative, governor, United States representative and senators, and President. A well-worded, concise letter is a valuable tool. On a more urgent and immediate issue, a telegram forcefully registers opinion. On the local level, a phone call can be helpful. A brief conference might be the most dramatic vehicle of influence, but make it short—no more than a few minutes. Keep in mind the old adage that wisdom has ten parts—nine are silence and the other is brevity. Politicians, a word which I use respectfully, will appreciate the fact that you value their schedule. Know what you want to say, say it, and keep on saying it in the future if the need continues.

Do you know that the exercise of influence is even closer to you than the office of the councilman, mayor, governor, etc.? You have loved ones, neighbors, and friends whom you can urge to join you. Best results come when you sensibly point out the needs as you see them and some solutions. If you don't have answers, try to find some. The person who always points out the problems and never offers any solutions is a problem himself! I suggest seven commandments for finding answers which you may recommend.

1. Admit that you are not a know-it-all. (The truth is, neither you, I, nor anyone else actually knows everything about anything!)
2. Gather all the information you can on the subject.
3. Consider *all* the facts which are at your disposal on the subject.
4. Ask for divine guidance in the matter.
5. Humbly receive clarity of thought from God to interpret the information.
6. Evaluate the information at hand.
7. Then act on the facts you have.

Invite your friends to share their opinions and ideas. Then request their help in dealing with policy makers. Influence is a "we" proposition. You are probably aware of the old story about the weakness of a single thread. It has little power. But put fifty strings of thread together and they can bind a big object.

Older people possess the ability to participate in processes of government. Already the retired segment of our society has immense political clout within its grasp. As the older-person population explosion accelerates, the possibility to exercise power increases. Use it for good by involving yourself in the processes available to you!

As one person, you can count. Sir Michael Costa, the renowned conductor, rehearsed with a large orchestra and a choir consisting of several hundred singers. As the pipe organ thundered and the drums rolled, a piccolo player thought, "With all this noise, my little instrument doesn't make any difference." He stopped playing.

Suddenly, Sir Michael gave the cue for the music to halt. Everything was quiet when he cried, "Where is the piccolo?" [2]

You may be like the piccolo player, but just as the piccolo is vital to the orchestra, you are important to government. Withdrawal withers you as a person and reduces the effectiveness of government toward you, older people as a group, and society at large.

However, the answer to integration into society lies in more than participation in the processes of government. Since your life must *not* be lived in isolation, it includes involvement with others, the impetus for which must come from within you. A more thorough integration can be accomplished in the course of everyday living.

MAKE YOURSELF "OTHERABLE"

To successfully interact with those around you, make yourself "otherable." What do I mean by "otherable"? An "otherable person" is one who more easily relates to other people, who has the ability to be a group person and still maintain his own individuality. This requires skill in the art of human relationships and clever control of emotions and tongue. To develop as an "otherable" person, you begin with yourself.

1. Stop Fearing Life

As an older person, you may have acquired a certain fear of life. This affects you emotionally, spiritually, and possibly physically. Assuredly, it affects your relationship to others because the fear-spirit will leap from one person to another unless it is rejected.

The negative power of such fear is demonstrated by the story of a man who opened a small restaurant. As the business prospered, he enlarged the restaurant to seat one hundred people. Then he opened one at a new location. In a few years, the man owned ten successful restaurants.

When his son graduated from high school the man was overjoyed. Since he had been denied a college education, he had dreamed about the boy going to a fine school. Now he was able to send him. He imagined the day when they would become business partners—a father-son team. Oh, the happiness of the man was without limits!

His son received his degree and joined his father in the restaurant business. At that time, the country was in the throes of a recession. "Dad," said the son, "you know, the nation is in a slump. Business is bad. Things are tough. Companies are going under. Now, we've got to cut back on advertising and let some of our workers go. We've got to tighten our belts and pull in the reins."

Although there was a general economic slow-down, the father's business had been steadily increasing. But his son was an "educated" man. He had completed many courses in management and marketing. His handsomely-framed degree in Business Administration proved it.

The father thought, "You know, my son has something. All this time, we've been in a slump and I didn't know it!" Fear jumped on his mind like a starved lion. They cut back, cut down, and eventually closed their doors!

This basic fear has a splitting effect on relationships. As an unseen spiritual force, it erects barriers between one another when the need is to build bridges to each other.

2. Stop Fussing

An argumentative person doesn't win friends and influence people. He repels them and then soaks in his own misery. I confess that you can always find many circumstances in a world like ours over which to fuss. For example, Dick Richards, a man I am privileged to know, is sixty-seven years old. For thirty-one of those years, he has been totally blind. At age forty-four, he became completely deaf. But in the past eighteen years, Dick has become an accomplished violinist and historian. Many schools for handicapped children call on him for assistance. On numerous occasions, he has been invited to address historical societies. Dick could have capitulated to adverse conditions. Instead, he has claimed and captured them to benefit himself and others. I have never met a man with a more pleasant and winsome personality.

Possibly you have noticed that the people who tell you something for your own good seldom have anything good to tell you! At best, "he has a right to censure who has a heart to help," as William Penn once said.[3]

Do you want to be around fussy people? Of course, you don't. Now, apply to yourself what you want others to be around you.

3. Stop Fooling

It was quite an experience for me to walk through a museum of natural history and carefully look over the different kinds of animals. They appeared to be real. The whale, the lion, the eagle, the wolf, the hummingbird—each seemed to be perfectly alive. But the whale spouted no water, the lion did not roar, the eagle did not soar away, the wolf failed to howl, and the hummingbird gathered no nectar. They were lifeless and motionless because they were stuffed. Outside the museum, they would have fooled me.

"Fool" in Latin means "windbag." It also means to deceive, to be a hypocrite. Now, that is an interesting word. "Hypo" signifies "under," and "crite" refers to "dispute" or "contend." Combine the two and you have one who contends against (under) you while he maintains a show for you. As they rode through a cheering throng, Lord Cromwell said to Fairfax, "They would turn out with the same enthusiasm to see me hanged."

South American Indians call a hypocrite "a man with two faces," "a man with two hearts," "a man with two kinds of talk," "a two-headed person," "a two-sided man," "a person with a straight mouth and a crooked heart." Anyone like this is unreal on the inside; therefore, he is not capable, in that condition, to be an "otherable" person except to those who likewise are unreal. Even then the foundation is like a paper tiger. It will quickly cave in or blow away.

4. Get Along With Yourself

This is one of the basic rules for an "otherable" person: You will get along with others to the degree that you get along with yourself! Anybody who doesn't enjoy a meaningful relationship with himself is incapable of establishing and maintaining happy relationships with other people. The principle at work is that how we look at others is shaped by our own attitudes.

Two ministers were asked what kind of congregations they served. One said, "Horrible! Terrible! I've been there ten years and I can't stand them anymore." Someone asked, "What's wrong?" He answered, "I have a congregation of Archie Bunkers. Blue-collar, cautious, bigoted, reactionary people who think that God is the American military-industrial complex."

The other minister replied, "I have an exciting church and I know that God is going to do a marvelous work in it and through it." He was asked to describe his congregation. "It's a church full of Archie Bunkers. I find beneath the surface there is pure gold. They are really the mainstream behind America's greatness. Full of courage, they work hard and they're faithful, loyal people. I believe that God's touch on my people will make the church alive and a mighty force in our city and denomination."

What difference was there between the two congregations as described? None. Why the opposite opinions by the ministers? What each one saw in his congregation was colored by what kind of person he was. It isn't any surprise what happened in the churches.

The wars between us are a show of the war within us. The outside is a reflection of the inside. I recall a man who was inhumanly crabby with fellow workers. That irritability with them showed the irritation on the inside with himself. Experience in you extends into life. Activity is established on inner experience, feelings, hopes, dreams. The glasses through which you see and treat others are your own.

5. Be Practical About Relationships

The "otherable" person need not be dismayed when he discovers that he doesn't click with everyone. Because people are people, misunderstandings arise. You are an individual and not a robot; consequently, differences will surface. Your own well-being and relationships with people depend on a practical approach. Allowances are made in scripture: "If possible, so far as it depends on you, live peaceably with all" (Rom. 12:18, RSV).

When a problem develops in a relationship, there is a course of action which may restore happiness.

1) *Approach the person:* The tendency is to shun him. A man whose business partner had betrayed him said, "If there's ever any reconciliation, *he's* going to take the first step!" The need is contact and the time to do it is now. *Who* takes the first step is of secondary importance. If you are aware of the problem, then you are responsible for approaching the individual.

2) *Be honest with the person:* Honesty is truth in a spirit of goodwill.

3) *Respect the feelings of the person:* This will help unwind the knot which has developed.

4) *Listen to the opinions of the person:* You will find out what he thinks only by listening to what he has to say. I heard a man say that home is where you can say whatever you please because no one is listening anyway. Such an attitude probably caused the unhappy relationship in the first place. At least, it fueled the problem. Listen!

5) *Use the method of reverse principle:* Instead of matching criticism with criticism, hate with hate, and fire with fire,

demonstrate the reverse of what the person shows. Returning negative kind only with negative kind lowers you to the level of your adversary.

6) *Keep "I'm sorry" ready for use:* That is one of the most powerful problem-solvers in your vocabulary.

A retired woman who has such healthy, happy relationships shared her secret. "I always try to light a candle rather than sweep out the darkness."

6. Share Efforts with People Your Own Age and Other Ages

Napoleon Hill wrote, "The real riches of life increase in exact proportion to the scope and extent of the benefit they bring to those with whom they are shared." [4] There is a special joy for those who act together. In addition, pulling in unison produces greater results.

Doing things with people of different ages causes an interaction that is beneficial to all who are involved. I remember a seventeen-year-old girl who spent more than two-thousand hours as a volunteer in a nursing home. One resident said, "We wouldn't want to live if Pam didn't come in." I am also acquainted with a couple in their sixties who continue to work with young people in a church. "Our youth add so much to our lives," the couple claims. Several generations of young people have come under their loving influence. Those who are in their group now wouldn't think of getting rid of the older couple.

At times it might be trying for people of various ages to work together. The cartoon "Little Emily" once showed a beauty salon with this sign in the window: Now! Ladies' hair dyed for $20. Two youngsters were reading it. One of them, a devilish-looking fellow, says, "I can turn it grey for less money than that!"

Life is an exciting affair when you unite in action with others. This helps you achieve integration into society. The joy comes when you put your powers to use in natural and helpful ways.

7. Spend One-Half Of Your Waking Hours With Others

How can you, an older person, expect to be a part of society, accepted as an individual, loved and appreciated and valued, when you put up the "by myself" roadblock? Separation from society is widened when you are a loner. Yet older people are inclined to retreat into a confined world of their own. And they are susceptible to a loneliness which plagues many retired persons.

Dr. Carl R. Rogers, a leading authority on human nature, wrote that there are two elements in this loneliness—an estrangement from one's self, and the absence of a relationship in which one can communicate his experiences with another.[5]

Younger people should be aware of this inclination and do what they can to encourage older persons to be with others. As a retiree, you can make sure that you spend one-half of your waking hours with others. Perhaps you feel you need more time with them. But remember that your family and friends have other commitments and interests. Do not necessarily feel that all of your time with others must be spent with the same people. If you are physically able, you can devote some time to older people who are confined to hospital or home. Younger people, too, would do well to invest time with seniors who are incapacitated and handicapped.

An older person who was bedridden told me, "Mr. Ray, no one ever calls me or comes to see me." There are two steps such a person can take. One is to phone your own church and let them know you will welcome visits from people of the congregation. Ask that someone call on you. Arrange for periodic visits. If you have no church home, phone one of your choice and request their help. Second, do what you can to make the visits a pleasurable experience for the ones who call. Welcome them graciously. You are glad to see them and you appreciate them for visiting you. Let it show!

Don't dampen the visit with exclamations of self-pity and negative conversation. Some older people have spewed out resentment and bitterness on visitors to the extent that the callers think, "Well, I never want to go there again!" You can share your feelings without becoming repulsive. Keep this question in mind: If you were the visitor and the visitor were you, would you enjoy visiting him?

Although the idea is to spend some time with others and avoid being alone all of the time, remember that no one wants to be with others *constantly* unless there is an abnormal need in his life. You deserve the quietness of some aloneness. Reflection and meditation are best accomplished away from the crowd. Vast spiritual strength is available during positive aloneness.

8. Think Now

Younger people are inclined to depend on the future, whereas older people are inclined to depend on the past. The difference between those trends of thought contribute to the separation of retirees from society. The blame is not totally on the hands of older persons, yet a retired person can help close the gap by thinking *now*.

You see, when anyone lives in the past, he goes downstream in life and stagnates. It is more than nostalgia. It is an overemphasis on the "good old days" which causes regressive behavior. Dominated by the past, retired people get the reputation of being "old fogies" and "yesterday's men."

Usually, the one who lives in the past is guilty of bloating the "good old days." Were they really as "good" as you think? A man says, "Well, I could buy a steak for a dime a pound." Does he remember that he had to work an hour for that dime, whereas now it takes less than fifteen minutes? How "good" were the sweat shops and sixty-six-hour workweeks? Today the average is less than forty! What about those days when, on the whole, there was lesser concern for human dignity and worth? Were they the days of law and order, or was lawlessness just unreported since there weren't televisions, radios, and newspapers on every corner? Furthermore, there were fewer people in those days and the statistics did not have the advantages of more sophisticated and reliable methods. As we move farther away from the past, the more our imagination works to unfocus the realities of that past.

As an older person, you don't need to cut the umbilical cord to your life which is rooted in yesterdays. *However, you do need to have your thinking dominated by the present hour.* Ralph Waldo Emerson commented on this when he said,

> One of the illusions of life is that the present hour is not the critical, decisive hour. Write it on your heart that every day is the best day of the year. He is rich, and he alone, who owns the day, and no one owns the day who allows it to be invaded with fret, worry, and anxiety.

Practice living in the present. It will bring you and other generations closer together.

9. Be Adjustable, Yet Firm

One of the surest facts of modern life is that society is changing. As I discussed in *The Art of Christian Meditation*, medical science and population are changing so rapidly that physicians and nations are taxed almost beyond their limits. The challenge to adjust causes great stress and disorientation.[6] As I wrote this chapter, I received updated information from the United States Census Bureau. Since 1970, the population of people sixty-five years of age and older in the Southern states has increased a whopping 22.1 percent.[7] W. R. Inge, the American clergyman, summarized it by saying that when our first parents were driven out of Paradise, Adam remarked to Eve, "My dear, we live in an age of transition." [8]

When Nehru was India's leader, he stated, "It is curious how age seems to have the same effect on a people or a race as it has on an individual—it makes them slow of movement, inelastic in mind and body, conservative, and afraid of change." [9] This rigidity and inflexibility among older persons causes an isolation from the society that is in process of change. Possibly many retirees feel like the woman who said, "I can't keep up." Another stated, "I'm part of another era." Someone else remarked, "Frankly, I don't intend to adapt."

A certain and positive adjustability is not only required, it is wholesome. As Kakuzo Okanura pointed out, "The art of life lies in a constant readjustment to our surroundings." [10] However, not *every* change our society is undergoing is worthwhile. Some, such as a relaxation of morality, runs smack up against truth, conscience, and pure principles. In these cases, a positive and firm nudging by older persons can help society get on track. However, when truth is not the issue, it is wise to be more flexible.

TEN COMMANDMENTS OF HUMAN RELATIONS

Someone sent me a copy of the Ten Commandments of Human Relations by an unknown author. They summarize and reemphasize points for an "otherable" person and I believe they are a fitting climax to this chapter.

1) Speak to people. There is nothing so nice as a cheerful word of greeting.

2) Smile at people. It takes seventy-two muscles to frown, only fourteen to smile.

3) Call people by name. The sweetest sound to anyone's ears is the sound of his own name.

4) Be friendly and helpful. If you would have friends, be friendly.

5) Be cordial. Speak and act as if everything you do were a genuine pleasure.

6) Be genuinely interested in people.

7) Be generous with praise—cautious with criticism.

8) Be considerate of the feelings of others. It will be appreciated.

9) Be thoughtful of the opinions of others. There are three sides to a controversy—yours, the other fellow's and the right one.

10) Be alert to give service. What counts most in life is what we do for others.

8.

Positive Attitude—
Personal Altitude

"Whatever that be which thinks,
understands, wills, and acts, it
is something celestial and divine."
        —Cicero

As Grandma on "The Waltons" television show, Ellen Corby said, "You must have enthusiasm for life or life is not going to have a lot of enthusiasm for you." Truer words were never spoken, especially from an older person to older people!

Enthusiasm for life is mainly a matter of attitude. Sometime ago, I attended a birthday party for an eighty-four year old woman in my congregation. It was a joyful occasion because the one being honored exuded sincere enthusiasm for life. As my wife and I left, I leaned over to this delightful person and said, "I hope to see you on your birthday next year." She replied, "I don't see any reason you shouldn't. *You* look pretty healthy to me." At eighty-four, with various ailments that afflict older people, she had personal altitude through wholesome attitude. Yet, as a leading physician, himself past sixty-five, said to me, "It's so common for seniors to fall into a consistent pattern of negativism." Some realize this weakness and wonder what can be done about it.

At a workshop, I asked the people to write in two sentences or less what they believe to be their greatest need. To encourage them to be completely honest in their answer, I assured them that no one would see what they wrote. They could fold up the slip of paper and take it home with them.

Afterwards, eight people who were sitting together came to

113

me and said that they shared with one another what they had written. To their surprise, each one, independently, had listed an improved attitude.

Let's define attitude as a prevailing frame of mind—your mental posture. Like the moon is a reflection of the sun, attitude is the reflection of the most dominant and consistent thoughts. It must be admitted that your attitude is a powerful force in your life.

I received in the mail a page torn out of a magazine. At the top, it has the heading of: "Are There Two Of You?" Below it: "Love Your Neighbor." Then, under this, it shows two faces, back-to-back, of a single man. One is smiling and captioned: "Love Your Neighbor." The other is frowning like that of a bearish grouch. It is captioned: "Business is business." "Get while the getting is good." "It's dog eat dog." "If I don't, somebody else will." The question posed is, "Why do so many of us think one way on weekends and another way when we go back to work on Monday?" [1] This ad infers a split personality, or a divided self, which is but the product of a "Split Attitude"—a frame of mind that is untamed, unorganized, unsynthesized, and unchanneled.

There are eight significant points I wish to bring out:

1. Your Life Is Determined by Your Attitude

You may be like an automobile—right at home on the uphill climb, or running smoothly only going downhill, or perhaps both. But everything depends on your attitude. I saw this truth at work in a youngster who appeared to be about ten years old.

During a week of heavy rains, I drove past the boy as he laboriously tried to get his kite up in the air. It wasn't actually raining at the time, but it had been, and it was cloudy, overcast, damp, and dreary—not much of a day for kite-flying. Yet one thing was sure: In his heart, the sun was out. I could have stopped my car and said, "Say, fellow, don't you know this isn't kite-flying weather? You'll never get it up today!" And he could have replied, "Mister, what's wrong with today?

Watch me." In his mind, the day was suitable for kite-flying. And he got the kite up.

It is mostly a person's frame of mind which makes or breaks daily life. Yes, attitude is the great key, even for older people.

In 1928, a mechanic in Washington, D.C. replied to a reporter's question about Oliver Wendell Holmes. "Justice Holmes? He's the young judge who's always upsetting the old guys on the Supreme Court." At the time the amazing Mr. Holmes, Chief Justice of the Supreme Court, was eighty-seven years old! As one of my parishioners said:

> You are as young as your faith,
> As old as your doubt,
> As young as your self-confidence,
> As old as your fear,
> As young as your hope,
> As old as your despair.

2. Attitude And Actuality Are Brothers

What you think either dictates or influences what happens. Unfortunately, a critical-minded individual brings forth criticism toward and from others by the very nature of his attitude. An attitude of fault-finding will seek out faults.

The invisible chemistry at work here and its root cause is mentioned by Hornell Hart. After a thorough study, Dr. Hart concluded:

For a large majority of those who lack comradeship the reason is not in the antagonisms of their associates; it is not the misfortune that places them in the midst of unfriendly folks; it is not that they happen to be working under tyrannical, unsympathetic, and emotionally maladjusted chiefs; it is not that there are conspiracies against them. For the great majority of people who lack comradeship the reason is inherent in certain basic qualities in themselves.[2]

There is a bond of cooperation between attitude and reality by which they supply each other. Dominant thoughts provoke action; that is, you act the way you think. Then, action crystalizes attitude. For instance, the older man with a victorious frame of mind insisted that the problem he encountered would be resolved. He thought and acted in a manner which showed his attitude. When the problem was resolved, his attitude was reinforced.

3. Attitude Needs Facts, Not Suppositions

Many older people have fallen prey to suppositions about diminished capabilities inflicted on them by the years. "I can't think for myself" and "I'm unable to do this." These are products of the helplessness syndrome. What about the taboo in regards to sexual activity?

Another common supposition concerns the quality of life in a day of rapid inflation (over six percent annually from 1950–1977, with medical expenses one thousand percent higher during the same period), high taxes, and fixed income. Of course, to many older people, finances are a serious problem. "You know," said a retiree, "the dollar won't buy what it used to." That is right, but there are more resources now than in the past.

According to Senator William Proxmire, since 1960 the average American has increased his purchasing power by forty percent, despite inflation and taxes. The number of statistically poor families has dropped by a third and the American economy has created twenty million new jobs.[3]

Facts can startle us! If your attitude functions on incorrect suppositions, your actions will be faulty. Negative suppositions create a sour frame of mind.

4. Attitude and Sense of Purpose Are Inseparable

Albert W. Bell, a leader in the black community of Jackson, Mississippi, and a friend of mine, made a speech in which he said, "Meet me at no special place and I will be there at no particular time." In the talk, he pointed out that purposeless living reflected by that statement plagues many people with whom he has contact. This plague is not confined to Mr. Bell's community. It is a major affliction of older people.

Dr. Teilhard de Chardin explained the role of purpose. "A man will continue to research only so long as he is prompted by some passionate interest, and this interest will be dependent on the conviction, strictly undemonstrable to science, that the universe has a direction." [4]

It is direction, or sense of purpose, as a part of attitude which gives the attitude a chance to show itself. If significant purpose in your life is unrealized, you are working with a minimized frame of mind. The flow back to your mind from purposelessness further deteriorates attitude.

5. Attitude Shapes Response

Anyone who has the capacity to think is capable of responding to others and to the turns of events which may happen in his life. However, the nature of his response depends on his attitude toward life, on the larger scale, and on the person or event to which he responds, on a limited and more personalized scale. I am thinking of the response of a physician who was approached by an older woman. In distress over getting older, she asked, "Doctor what can I do with my grey hair?" He answered, "Admire it." He, too, was an older person with a head covered by grey hair. The attitude he possessed about aging conditioned and pleasantly flavored his response to the lady's question.

6. Attitude Is Shaped by Response

Yes, attitude shapes response. And yes, attitude is shaped *by* response because it is a two-way street.

A grandfather told me about the day he was asked to stay with six grandchildren while their parents went shopping. Since the grandmother had other commitments, he had to tackle the task single-handedly. Four hours later, the parents returned. Flustered and bewildered, granddad was standing at the door waiting to hand them a record of events. The list read:

Dried the children's tears—22 times
Wiped their noses—13 times
Separated them—17 times
Tied their shoestrings—16 times
Got them drinks of water—24 times
Told them to "hold it down"—23 times
Said, "Don't do that," "Quit it," and "Leave them alone"—29 times
Balloons blown—3 per child
Average life of balloon—12 seconds
Cautioned children not to cross the street—34 times
Children insisted on crossing the street—34 times
Number of times Grandpa will do this alone in the future—0

The man's response affected his attitude (number of times Grandpa will do this alone in the future—0).

7. Attitude Is Affected by Physical Condition

Probably you have heard all those claims that the mind rules over matter. To a point, this is true. Most people, including seniors, could improve themselves immensely by developing the larger powers of their minds. They would discover an amazing dominance of mind over matter. Yet, there is a relationship between mind and matter which makes physical condition an influential partner on attitude.

For instance, a tired body eventually will wear down your processes of thought. The body requires adequate rest through which its strength is rejuvenated and restored. Physical exhaustion strains mental functions.

Dr. John E. Gibson states that a person should postpone doing critical work or making important decisions when he is in a frustrated state of mind. In this condition, a person is robbed of mental horsepower and his ability to think and reason are hampered. Researchers at Ohio University found that "frustrated subjects make significantly more errors than non-frustrated subjects." [5]

This reference is just as accurate when applied to extreme tiredness. Apparently, Thomas A. Edison, the phenomenal American inventor, knew this and abode by it.

Mrs. Edison said of her husband, "He could work hard and long, then lie on his old couch and go immediately to sleep. He was like a child in God's hands—nature's man. Perhaps this was one reason God could pour all these wonderful ideas through his mind." [6]

8. Attitude Can Be Changed

Your attitude results from a collection of past and present experiences, to which you have responded in some manner. *Immediate environment* and *people* (like close friends, wife, husband, children, mother, father, sisters, and brothers) are powerful inputs to attitude.

We are led to believe that over eighty percent of a person's attitude formed in the first seven years of his life stays with him for as long as he lives and substantially affects him unless he changes it. In a speech, a public opinion analyst stated that rebellious outbursts by the younger generation in the 1960s pointed to the thwarted attitudes of their parents. [7]

I talked with a sixty-year-old man who had no confidence. One reason was that when he was a child, his parents did over, and better, anything which he attempted. A seventy-one-year-old woman possessed an ample portion of ill-will toward her sister, who had taken her share of the family estate. Although it had happened twelve years before, the ill-will had grown to the extent that she was a most unhappy person.

Significant conditions (those to which you seriously relate because you perceive that they directly affect you) contribute to the formation of attitude. Vivian Hayes, R. N., who works with the outreach program for the elderly at the University of Notre Dame, refers to such conditions as loneliness, isolation, and loss of job and purpose in living. [8]

Hopes and dreams for today and the future (or a sense of

hopelessness and stagnation) have their way in the formulation of attitude. I am acquainted with an older couple who has great plans for the future. Their frame of mind is enlightened; they expect to realize their hopes.

In the final analysis, however, *your attitude is what you make it and allow it to become.* The ultimate decision is on your hands, for much of the time the catalyst which results in a turn of events comes from you. Of course, this is not true all the time—no one chooses to have leukemia. But in every situation you are responsible for your response.

MAINTAINING A POSITIVE ATTITUDE

Hopefully, you now see just how important your attitude in older age is, and that it can be changed. Then you are ready to begin an eight-step improvement process which will lead *you* to personal altitude through positive attitude:

1. Pull the Plug on Negative Feelings

Dr. James Melvin, a physician, personal friend, and older person of whom I spoke in a previous chapter, introduced me to Murphy's Laws. They include:

If anything can go wrong, it will.

When it does go wrong, it will happen to you.

If there is a possibility of several things going wrong, the one that goes wrong is the one that will do the most damage.

If everything seems to be going well, you have overlooked something.

Nothing ever quite works out.[9]

There is a lot of humor in these laws, but they cease to be funny when people believe them to the extent that they accept and apply them in life. When this happens, the laws represent a sinister pessimism. Pessimism, according to Samuel J. Hurwitt, is the seed from which calamity sprouts.[10]

The older person needs to be free from pessimism. It saps away creative and problem-solving forces. He has enough challenges from outside himself which require all the spiritual and mental powers he can muster.

If you talk and act predominantly from negative feelings, you probably have a sense of dissatisfaction which gnaws at your insides, much like a small scrub and a tall pine tree. The scrub looked at the ground and whimpered, "Look how short I am." The towering pine looked at the sky and lamented, "Look how short I am." An optimist is one who welcomes the boom which may follow the last recession, whereas the pessimist points out that the boom is only a prelude to the next recession. Do you see the difference? Yet, as Gloria Pitzer claimed, "Few cases of eyestrain have been developed by looking on the brighter side of things." [11]

When negative feelings inordinately influence a person, the spillover affects those around him. As a pessimist, he usually sees first the dark side of the other person's problems. Consequently, he is apt to be a discouraging factor.

Negative feelings seem to have a more fertile field among older persons. Maybe the reasons involve an accumulation of bad experiences (I deal with this later in the process), responses to perceived injustices toward you as an older person, and a blatant failure to recognize the preciousness of life and the enriching opportunities now at your fingertips. At any rate, the toll on you is lower-level living, and you must shed the control those negative feelings have over you.

2. Practice Positive Imagination

There is within us the capacity for and a tendency to become like that which we imagine ourselves to be. Fear of old age, retirement, dependency, aloneness, senility, unwantedness, and death are results of imagination. The nature of your reply to the following questions mainly reflects what use you make of imagination:

1. When faced with a problem for which you have no answer on hand, do you say, "Let's find the answer" or "Nobody knows"?
2. When you make a mistake, do you say, "I was wrong" or "It wasn't my fault"?
3. When there is a flaw in your character, do you say, "I'm okay, but not as good as I can be" or, "I'm not as bad as some people I know"?
4. Do you try to learn from others or do you try to tear them down?
5. Do you say, "Let's find a better way" or "This is the way it has always been done"?

You see, more minds rust out than wear out because imagination is unused, underused, and wrongly used. An unemployed imagination is an unenjoyed imagination. John Quincy Adams, the sixth President of the United States, appropriately stated that old minds are like horses; you must exercise them if you wish to keep them in working order.[12]

The secret to wholesome attitude is to practice positive imagination. This is a redeemed and redeeming use of it. John Ruskin expressed the idea when he said, "Make yourselves nests of pleasant thoughts, bright fancies, satisfied memories, noble histories, faithful sayings, treasure-houses of restful thoughts." [13]

For the older person, a mile walk each day with his imagination is an unequalled experience—as long as the images used are on the upgraded side!

3. Self-Management

One of the unique powers still available to older people is to manage their own lives as much as possible. Two incidents come to mind which illustrate the need for and results of self-management.

After a long illness, Katherine's husband passed away. She was grief-stricken and felt she couldn't go on in life without him, yet she was only fifty-five years of age and quite attractive. Katherine could have met the need and plodded ahead with the business of living. Instead, she retreated. When her friends invited her out, she declined. Organizations in which she had been active asked her help, but she refused, insisting that she didn't have the energy and "I don't feel like it." For three years, she lost the power of self-management. Although this isn't uncommon when a spouse dies, it is unnecessary. Happily, she eventually realized life must continue and it can be good. From that point, Katherine began to live again with a renewed enjoyment of her life. She gained a fresh vitality for activities. An annoying feeling of fatigue mysteriously disappeared.

I cherish my friendship with an eighty-six-year-old woman who summarized her secret of self-management.

1. Laugh at difficulties. (She finds they disappear.)
2. Attempt heavy responsibilities. (She finds they grow lighter.)
3. Face bad situations with courage. (She finds they clear up.)
4. Tell the truth. (She finds it more rewarding.)
5. Believe others are honest. (She finds that most of them live up to that expectation.)
6. Trust God every day. (She finds him surprising her constantly with his loving goodness.)
7. Keep your mind on God. (She finds mental and spiritual peace that way.)

The effort to control yourself and your own affairs reassures the attitude that you and life are worthwhile. It enlarges a good feeling of personal pride. It also releases energy by which to meet the many demands of living as an older person. The positive influence it exerts on attitude is evident by the confidence that you will have available whatever you need, at the time you need it, to keep your life meaningful and adequate.

To accomplish self-management, keep in mind that when faced with heavy events and circumstances, powerful problems, and unlikeable characteristics in yourself or others, the word "impossible" really means that realization of a certain dream, objective, and aspiration requires more than what you see as the available resources. It does *not* mean that you are

denied the resources! Look for the possibility in every im-
possibility. It is there! Someone told me, "If you are willing
to die for it, there is nothing you cannot accomplish." The
impossible can be done when men and mountains meet. Yes,
when you maintain control of the mountain by self-management!

4. Use the Law of Mental Substitution

There are times in the life of every person, especially older
folk, when inferior thoughts need to be substituted with
superior thoughts. Simply stated, this law is the art of replace-
ment.

A few minutes ago, my secretary told me that a gentleman
asked to see me. When he introduced himself, I recognized
the name as one of the most prominent businessmen in the
Southern states. "I've come without an appointment," he explained. "In fact, I didn't know that I would drive by your
office until a few minutes ago."

In his fifties, the man shared the heartbreaking news that
his twenty-six-year-old son had gone to the doctor a few
weeks ago, thinking he might have some manageable stomach
ailment. They discovered cancer that had already advanced
to the inoperable stage. At the moment, he is at one of the
nation's leading centers for treatment of cancer, where he is
undergoing extensive cobalt treatments.

The father described his deep concern for his son, fifteen-
month-old grandson, and daughter-in-law. "He's such a bright,
outgoing young man with a great future ahead of him. He's a
natural-born leader. At the university, he was one of the
most popular and respected students on campus. He loves life
and people. People love him. He's a fine Christian and devoted
churchman. I told him that if it were within my power, I'd
trade places with him. He replied, 'I know you would, Dad.' "
In a hushed manner, the father said, "I've never met you until
now. All I want to ask is that you pray for my son."

I assured him that my entire congregation would remember both the son and the family. "However, I will remind my

people that, when they pray, they should replace thoughts of death with thoughts of God's power, and love, and providence. That rather than think about weakness, they should think about the strength available for your son and the family to meet the hour. Instead of disease, I shall prompt them to think about health."

This is a use of the law of substitution. It doesn't deny reality; it saves it and places it on a higher level. When you are sad, think about something which can generate a happy feeling. When a turn of events tends to pull you apart, think about a beautiful and quiet place you have visited where you felt unified. When you begin to feel you haven't enough resources to take care of your needs, substitute a thought of prosperity and hold on to it.

In itself, the substitution will not totally satisfy every need, but it will help get the forces in motion, including yourself, by which to cope with and meet the need.

5. Establish Peace with the Past

Coming to terms with the past is one of the most serious challenges on your hands. And a wholesome attitude will not be experienced unless you start doing it. The years on your life-meter have some failures and surely some disappointments. Numerically, you probably have more years behind you than in front of you, so you have had much time to develop a past. Unhandled, that which has happened crams your mind with cynicism, resentments, doubt, fears, and "I wish I'd done this instead of that." Older people who succumb to such stuff are already dead and might not know it. Most of all, their existence is more tragedy than triumph.

On the other hand, an individual can establish peace with the past and come out of it a much better and happier person. The company for which a sixty-year-old man worked closed its operation in his city. He was an able, cheerful, creative, energetic worker—the kind the boss likes to keep on the job. Besides, he had twenty-four years seniority. When the plant was closed, he got six months salary and a slap on the back.

"I began looking for another job," he said, "feeling that I had some good productive years left for some company who needed my services. But I was systematically, politely, firmly turned down." After four months, he began to take on a sense of despair. "I felt rejected. You know," he stated, "it's an awful feeling to think you're unwanted.

"I asked myself, 'Norman, are you going to fall into hopelessness and give up?' I decided, 'No!' So I kept going." He has now completed eight wonderful years for a boss who appreciates contribution and is not biased by chronology.

The peace the man established with the past (the unfortunate closing of his old company) came when he stood up to that turn of events and committed himself to keep going.

An experience I had while visiting in a hospital shows the effect of past events. There were two patients in the room, one of whom was a member of my church. Before leaving, I was requested to lead in a prayer. The other patient had kept one ear tuned in on the discussion, apparently. When she heard that we were about to have prayer, she said, "Reverend, will you say it loud enough so I can hear?"

I replied, "Of course. What's your name?"

"Rachel."

"And what's your ailment?"

"A stroke," she answered tearfully. "I've been here since Saturday . . . My left side is partially paralyzed . . . and I haven't taken it very gracefully." This new friend admitted that she was a captive of a low frame of mind which covered the entire spectrum of her existence; she was down on herself, the hopes of recovery, the stroke, and God.

To establish peace with your past, *accept what you are unable to change.* The sixty-year-old man whose company shut down operations in his city could not reverse that unexpected development. He exercised the only option available to him—which was to accept it.

I must remind you, however, that some of the past is changeable. Therefore, *change what you can.* Compare this to building a house. If a room is too small, it can be enlarged. Knock out an existing wall and extend the flooring.

Surely *you can resolve that the past will never be allowed to destroy you.* Such resolve is a set of the mind influenced by spiritual forces within you.

Art Fleming was the impressive host of television's "Jeopardy" show. I enjoyed watching that program when I could because of Art and the educational value of the show itself. I also had a personal interest in that Art is a committed Christian, a member and deacon in a church pastored by a friend of mine. For eleven years, "Jeopardy" enjoyed top ratings on daytime TV. Suddenly the network, without cause or reason, cancelled "Jeopardy." Art Fleming responded, "I really believe that every time one door closes, another—even a better one—opens. . . . I'm not the least bit upset about it. In fact, I can't wait to see what God has in store for me. My life is in the Lord's hands, and knowing that gives me the peaceful attitude I need. I can accept whatever he has in store for me and, whatever it is, it'll be better than 'Jeopardy'—I just know it." Art went on to say, "I don't claim to be 'holier than thou,' but I believe that if God is for me, who can be against me? My inspiration and guidance come from my everyday conversations with God. I thank him for each day—regardless of what happens. . . . God watches out for me. When things go wrong, he's not punishing us—he's strengthening us for even better things to come."

There is also peace with the past when you *use the past as a springboard to better your life now.* I remember the wise advice offered to me at a time when it appeared that unfortunate developments surrounding my life threatened me as a person and my future. The man said, "Dave, drive on. The past serves a better purpose when you move ahead from it."

The best thing a batter can do when he strikes out is to get up to the plate the next time around. The best thing a golfer can do after he drubs a shot is to walk over to the ball and calmly hit it again. The best thing a fisherman can do after he reels in the line and it's empty is to cast out the line again. A man I know has a simple yet remarkable way of doing just that.

In his office, he has two wastebaskets. One is by his desk,

as you would expect. The other is by the door. He says that the wastebasket is one of the greatest inventions of man, and that the one he has placed by his door is by far and away the most important item in his office. Above that basket is a calendar which shows the date for one day at a time. The last thing he does each evening before leaving the office is to stop at that basket. He tears off the sheet for that particular day, wads it up good, and drops it in the basket. He bows in prayer. What does he say? Something like this. "Heavenly Father, thank you for this day. I've done the best I know with it, but I'm sure I've done some dumb things. I've had some disappointments, but, Lord, it's now night. Forgive me. I move on. You gave me today. I now give it back to you with thanks. I expect tomorrow to be better."

In this sense, the past is left behind. You outlive yesterday. One of the best facts about the past is that it is past.

6. Be Selective in Your Responses

Successful living as an older person depends as much on your responses to what happens to you as on taking initiative by which results are more predictable. Your response is determined by your attitude. A wholesome attitude requires that you be selective in your responses.

I know a man whose wife was brutally and senselessly murdered. He said that he doesn't believe that everything which happens to us is for our good. Nevertheless, since the death of his wife, he is able to advise people in sorrow in ways he had never thought of before she was killed. The friend's response is selective.

The power of choice which makes it possible for a person to select a certain response is uniquely the possession of human personality. G. K. Chesterton used to say, "No one asks a puppy what kind of dog it means to be when it grows up." Such animals don't choose the ends they will pursue, but people do. It is in this power of choice that a person finds the responsibility to exercise the manner in which he will respond. Let me be quite specific.

Do you find pleasure when you see a beautiful red rose,

or do you complain because the rose has thorns? The rose, like life, has both—beauty and thorns. To you, the meaning of the rose, like life, is determined by your response.

In the 1940's, Walter Davis was the world's greatest high jumper. This accomplishment was even more amazing since he had suffered from polio as a youngster. You remember the iron lung into which victims were placed. One of the effects polio had on Walter was to wither his legs. But he courageously committed himself to develop his legs so that they would become strong and vigorous. There was the element of selective response. He could have resigned himself to his condition saying, "Oh, look at me. I have polio. I'll spend the rest of my life in an iron lung." This, too, would have constituted a response—one of defeat and devastation.

For ten years, Walter wore braces and underwent every kind of therapy at his disposal. Years later, he startled the world of sports by exceeding six feet, eleven and five-eighths inches, with room to spare!

I admit that some things which happen to older people and some things which are said to older people are unwanted and unexpected. At the same time, I must insist that the response you make to these is within your ability to control.

7. Unhurried Living

It may seem strange that in retirement, when people have time to enjoy life at a more leisurely stroll, there is a need to be reminded to slow down the pace. In short, snappy verse, Virginia Brazier wrote:

> This is the age
> Of the half-read page,
> The quick hash
> And the mad dash
> The bright night
> And the nerves tight,
> The plane hop
> And the brief stop
> The brain strain
> And the heart pain,

The cat nap
Till the spring snaps—
Then comes taps.

The system of rush-rush has developed during the working years. A pattern has been established and it will continue unless it is changed. I have met older people who feel a sense of guilt if they are not busy all the time. Their sense of well-being seems to be measured by constant and rapid activity. A man in his late sixties was hospitalized with a bladder problem. He told me, "I can't stand this place. Imagine having to waste these days lying here."

Such an approach is common among people in the industralized nations, yet it is unnatural and it needs to be altered. There's a story about some Americans who traveled through Africa.

When they began, they employed some natives to help and they told the natives that they were in a big hurry. The first day they rushed into the jungle. The second day they maintained a feverish pace through the jungle. On the third morning, the Americans were ready to start another frenzied day, but the Africans refused to budge. They simply squatted under some trees. "What's wrong," asked the Americans. The head native answered, "Today we shall rest to let our souls catch up with our bodies."

At its core, the problem of hurried living is a condition of the attitude. You feel you have got to keep on the go because your mind is set in that "go-go" direction. Attitude is the victim, especially at your age. Now, to reset this frame of mind, slow down your life. Take more time to eat. Spend a little more time in the shower or bath. Pace yourself when shaving and dressing to take longer. In the normal routine of walking, slow down the steps. Don't drive quite as fast as you used to. Spend a few more minutes with a friend. Arrange your schedule so that you can take more time to mow your yard, cultivate your garden, and putter in your garage workshop.

In previous years, you may not have noticed the beautiful blue sky and billowy cumulus clouds. You didn't pay any attention to the lovely flowers in the yards on your street. Life was mostly business. You were so busy making a living that you may have forgotten to make a life. As you neared older years, you might have feared aging and worried about the future to the extent that you overlooked the little things which add much to life.

In retirement, there is time to reduce the schedule to an enjoyable scale. Deliberate efforts will help you to develop the wholesome attitude that can make your life a joy.

8. Get a Good Laugh Every Day

There are two ways to look at this idea. First, laughter shows an attitude which conquers realities. Secondly, the lack of laughter shows realities which conquer attitude. Then, how can laughter affect attitude? Like the previous suggestion, a conscious effort influences that invisible thing I call frame of mind. A physician where I live claims that people who laugh are almost always more energetic, creative, buoyant, and resolute in achieving their goals. They spread happiness all around them and they can better absorb the buffetings from life.

The Chicken or the Eagle

A wholesome attitude answers the questions: "Are your retirement years a calamity or a crown? As an individual, do you compare with the chicken or the eagle?" This latter question refers to a story a parishoner shared with me:

A man walked through the forest looking for any bird of interest he might find. He caught a young eagle, brought it home and put it among his chickens, ducks, and turkeys. He give it chicken food, although it was an eagle, the king of birds.

A few years later, a naturalist came to see the man. As they walked in the garden, the visitor said, "That bird over there is an eagle, not a chicken." "Yes," answered the owner, "but I have trained it to be a chicken. It is no longer an eagle. It is a chicken even though it measures eighteen feet from tip to tip of its wings." "No," said the naturalist, "it is an eagle still. It has the heart of an eagle and I will make it soar high into the heavens." The owner replied, "Not so. It's a chicken. It will never fly." They agreed to test it.

The naturalist picked up the eagle, held it high, and said loudly, "Eagle, thou art an eagle. Thou dost belong to the sky and not to this earth. Stretch forth thy wings and fly!" The eagle turned its head to the left, then to the right, then downward where it saw the chickens eating their food. It jumped down to join them in the meal.

"I told you it is a chicken," said the owner. "It will never fly." The naturalist insisted, "No, it is an eagle. Give it another chance tomorrow." The next day, he took the eagle to the top of the house and in great seriousness said, "Eagle, thou art an eagle. Stretch forth thy wings and fly!" Again, the bird saw the chickens feeding below and jumped down to join them. Repetitively, the owner stated, "I told you this eagle is a chicken and it will never fly." "Not so," replied the determined naturalist. "It is an eagle. It has the heart of an eagle. Give it one more chance and I will make it fly."

The following morning, the men arose early. The naturalist took the eagle away from all the houses, to the foot of a high mountain. The sun was beginning to peek over the horizon, tinting the top of the mountains with gold. Every crag seemed to dance in the joy of a beautiful morning. He carefully picked up the eagle and said, "Eagle, thou art an eagle! Thou dost belong to the sky and not to the earth! *Stretch forth thy wings and fly!"*

The eagle looked around. It trembled as if new life were coming to it, yet it did not fly. Then, the naturalist forced it to look straight at the sun. Suddenly, it stretched out its wings and with the mighty screech of a majestic eagle, it soared into the air, mounting higher and higher, never again to return. It was an eagle although it had been kept and tamed so long as a chicken!

As an older person, your *capacity* for positive attitude must be compared to the eagle. Personal altitude through positive attitude is yours for the taking.

Stretch forth thy wings and fly!

9.

Life! And Life After Life!

"Life is real! Life is earnest!
And the grave is not the goal."
—*Henry Wadsworth Longfellow*

You have reached what society labels as the "golden years," but your experience may cause you to think they are not so golden. Ralph Waldo Emerson said, "We don't count a man's years until he has nothing else to count." Perhaps that statement doesn't mean much to you. "I can't" has you tied down; "I'm not up to it" has a stranglehold on you. You have let yourself feel inferior to the younger crowd, so you are on the run. You have forced your thinking processes into a small corner, maybe even to quit. In a nutshell, you have thrown a devastating block on living! Life is more a problem than a pilgrimage. Life is a program instead of a powerhouse. With hands folded meekly and feet crossed, you sit back like a victim for the vulture, waiting for the curtains to fall. The best you seem to manage is a sniffle or two as you strain to keep your dentures in. You are walking into the sunset—sliding is more like it. An aura of doom has engulfed your attitude, a feeling that "this is the end." But wait a minute. The sunset can be beautiful! And beyond the sunset is sunrise —Sunrise Unlimited!

Now we are getting into one of the most crucial considerations which can be addressed in the life of an older person. It is spiritual wholeness for living *and* dying. I do not feel that the two can be divorced from each other. They are closely related and connected, especially at your age. One affects the other even though many people in industrialized nations have refused to admit it—at least openly. Let's begin with the profound and far-reaching question: Is there a life after death?

The Judeo-Christian tradition is very rich and forceful in its reply: yes, *there is life after all human activity on this earth ceases!* Within many of us, there is a deep longing to know that a life which is beautiful and purposeful does continue beyond the grave. Then the teachings clearly reflected in scripture are satisfying and reassuring. Here are only a few of the witnesses.

Daniel

Many of them that sleep in the dust of the earth shall awake, some to everlasting life, and some to shame and everlasting contempt. And they that be wise shall shine as the brightness of the firmament (12:2–3, KJV).

Isaiah

Yet we have this assurance: Those who belong to God shall live again. . . . Those who dwell in the dust shall awake and sing for joy! For God's light of life will fall like dew upon them! (26:19, LB).

David

Surely goodness and mercy shall follow me all the days of my life; and I shall dwell in the house of the Lord forever (Ps. 23:6, RSV).

Paul

If for this life only we have hoped in Christ, we are of all men most to be pitied (1 Cor. 15:19, RSV).

But in fact Christ has been raised from the dead, the first fruits of those who have fallen asleep. For as by a man came death, by a man has come also the resurrection of the dead (1 Cor. 15:20–21, RSV).

John

Then I saw a new heaven and a new earth; for the first heaven and the first earth has passed away. . . . And I saw the holy city, New Jerusalem, coming down out of heaven from God . . . (Rev. 21:1–2, RSV).

Martha

. . . I know that he [Lazarus] will rise again in the resurrection at the last day (John 11:24, RSV).

Jesus

. . . for the hour is coming when all who are in the tombs will hear his voice and come forth, those who have done good, to the resurrection of life, and those who have done evil, to the resurrection of judgment (John 5:28–29, RSV).

But that the dead are raised, even Moses showed, in the passage about the bush, where he calls the Lord the God of Abraham and the God of Isaac and the God of Jacob. Now he is not God of the dead, but of the living; for all live to him (Luke 20:37–38, RSV).

Each one I have mentioned may have looked upon continuing life from a slightly different perspective; however, the common element is the same. There is life after death!

We must admit that it is a conclusion drawn on the basis of a religious faith. I use faith to mean a reality perceived to occur at some point in the future, established on the witness of intelligent and respected forefathers. Nevertheless, this faith does not violate the processes of reason. It utilizes them and gives reason something which it desperately needs—*hope!* From such hope, reason can claim death as a good and victorious encounter between the manifestation of life in two spheres: natural (here) and supernatural (beyond here).

Jesus risked a great deal on the testimony of the faithful who had preceded him. He also risked much on the basis of his own life, which he believed could not and would not be terminated by the death-event. Furthermore, the Galilean went so far as to base life after death for his followers on whether he transcended human life with continuing and endless life: "Because I live, you will live also" (John 14:19, RSV). Therefore, to Christians, the belief in continuing life is just as trustworthy as Jesus Christ himself was trustworthy.

Up to this point, the question as to whether there is life after death has been approached from the standpoint of faith, using scripture. A hard-core realist wants measurable evidence. Does such evidence exist? Is it possible to substantiate the claim if it is separated from faith? In my opinion, the answer is persuasively yes! It is accomplished by verifiable, supportive, and corroborative reports about the resurrection of Jesus.

According to various accounts, Jesus made at least twelve appearances to human beings, after His crucifixion, over a period of forty days.

Mary Magdalene—John 20:11 ff.

Other women—Matthew 28:9–10.

Peter—Luke 24:34.

Cleopas and another person on the road to Emmaus—Mark 16:12 ff.

Twelve people—John 20:19.

Again, with Thomas present—John 20:26 ff.

An unspecified number of people—Luke 24:44 ff.

Seven people—John 21.

Five hundred people—Matthew 28:16 ff.

James—1 Corinthians 15:7.

Paul—1 Corinthians 15:9.

A tough-minded realist with a brilliant mind as well as a man of faith, Paul recognized the overwhelming evidence which a discerning scientist can accept; therefore, he asked his hearers, "How can some of you say that there is no resurrection of the dead?" (1 Cor. 15:12, RSV).

Think about it: Twelve times, forty days, different places, various people in groups as well as individuals numbering well over five hundred all total, and referred to in six books written by five authors!

But was Jesus clinically dead when his body was removed from the cross? The evidence is most impressive that, indeed, he was dead.

By his own admission—"He said, "It is finished"; and he bowed his head and gave up his spirit" (John 19:30 RSV).

Roman military commander—"And when the centurion, which stood over against him, saw that he so . . . gave up the ghost [spirit], he said, Truly this man was the Son of God (Mark 15:39, KJV).

Forces of nature (earthquake and darkness in midafternoon)— Matthew 27:51 ff.

Women including Mary Magdalene and Mary, the mother of James and John—Matthew 27:56 ff.

Antagonistic Multitude—Luke 23:48 ff.

Local Officials—John 19:31

Roman soldiers—John 19:32–33

Joseph of Arimathaea—Mark 15:42

Pilate, the Roman Governor—Mark 15:43 ff.

Nicodemus, a Jewish leader—John 19:39

When Dan Thrapp was Religion Editor for the *Los Angeles Times,* he stated, "Someone has said that the Christian —or his church—'believes' there is life after death, but cannot 'know' it because no one can know what lies beyond death. The Easter story negates that view. By his return, Jesus answered vividly, by his own experience, that there is life after death, and that it is good. That it is a life of awareness. The difficulty arises when men attempt to interpret their faith in terms of rational quality or intellect. Intellect tells them that, once an individual is dead, he remains so. Faith—and Scripture—tell him that this is not true.

"What reason do we have for believing in the Resurrection, aside from pure faith? Well, the record, for one thing. Evidence. A band of scattered, demoralized disciples, none apparently particularly sensitive or psychologically aware, abruptly became convinced, devoted founders of a worldwide faith, each of them revealing courage unto death, often an agonizing death by torture, for the total conviction that suddenly had overwhelmed them. No interpretation of the Resurrection as a misty, psychological dream or vision or opinion could account for that stupendous event. But the fact could. The fact of the Resurrection. The fact that was recorded by simple, earthy men in the New Testament, the fact that alone could generate their surge of faith, the fact that Christians have believed ever since." [1]

When we accept the proposition that life continues beyond death, we are immediately confronted with another question: What kind of life is it? Biblical accounts give us some clues:

1) *Perception:* In the case of Jesus, people recognized him after his resurrection, although some responded slowly. And he recognized the people. I do not say that this is evidence sufficient to draw a firm conclusion that people will recognize one another in the life after death; for instance, a husband and wife and parents and children. It was important for the Master's followers to have everlasting life confirmed to them in the most real ways possible. But it may indicate that we, too, will possess such a sense of perception.

2) *Spiritual Awareness:* John wrote, "Behold, the tabernacle of God is with men, and he will dwell with them, and they shall be his people, and God himself shall be with them, and be their God" (Rev. 21:3, KJV). Does this not indicate that people will be aware of God, as well as God aware of people?

3) *Sense of Knowledge:* Paul stated, "For [now] we know in part, and we prophesy [speak forth] in part. But when that which is perfect is come, then that which is in part shall be done away. . . . Now we see through a glass, darkly; but then face to face: now I know in part; but then shall I know even as also I am known" (2 Cor. 13:9–10,12, KJV). It

appears to me that the capacity for knowledge will be a part of our personality in the future life.

4) *Body:* Again, Paul, who witnessed, "As we have borne the image of the earthy [in this life], we shall also bear the image of the heavenly" (1 Cor. 15:19, KJV). This does not indicate a physical body which is subject to disease and decay, but a spiritual body. As Jesus said, "For in the resurrection they neither marry, nor are given in marriage, but are as the angels" (Matt. 22:30, KJV). The reference to a body does imply perfect form and personality.

5) *Feeling:* John shared, "God shall wipe away all tears from their eyes; and there shall be no more death, neither sorrow, nor crying, neither shall there be any more pain: for the former things are passed away" (Rev. 21:4, KJV). The causes for these responses are removed through human death. The indication is that there will not be any association with dying in any fashion. The parallel conclusion is that a condition of joy will exist in which we share complete jubilation. Therefore, in that sense, feeling will be experienced.

Is it any wonder that Paul's stimulating treatment of the great transition from humanity to spirituality effected through the death-event is climaxed by, "Thanks be to God, which giveth us the victory through our Lord Jesus Christ" (1 Cor. 15:57, KJV)?

I have no doubt but what Eleanor Campbell is in her eternal home with God this moment. I remember her graciousness of character, the beauty of her love, the smile on her face, the transformation in her soul, and her family's beginnings in my church. I recall how she struggled with her arthritic condition to get up the flight of stairs to be in the Chancel Choir. I remember how much she hoped the new plastic hip that replaced her knotted bones would make it possible for her to have more productive years. How she wished for the help she sought at a special clinic in Oregon where she died. During those final weeks, she gave much time to Bible reading and prayer. There were no TV, radio, or newspapers. Just quietness in the small town of Wheeler.

On the eve of her death, Portia, a lovely daughter, held

her mother's hand and with tears cascading down her cheeks, said, "Mom, isn't it encouraging to know God?" Eleanor leaned back a bit and answered, "Indeed, it is! He's everything there is to real life." Perhaps with a twinge of premonition, she continued, "And I'll be completely well in the morning." This is the spirit of creative dying which was meant by the hymnwriter George Mattheson when he penned:

> O Joy that seekest me through pain,
> I cannot close my heart to thee;
> I trace the rainbow through the rain,
> And feel the promise is not vain,
> That morn shall tearless be.[2]

At seven o'clock the next morning Eleanor Campbell was "completely well." I believe she had unearthed one of the most dynamic and enlightening principles of dying. It is: *Only when you are willing to let go with human life are you really equipped to hold on to life and meaningfully enjoy it!*

By spiritual wholeness, Eleanor found a concept for dying which was adequate to escort her through the traumatic experience. This is the vital link which connects humanity to eternalness without pulling apart the seams of life. Actually, it attracts life to a higher sphere where it is loved, cherished, used, and made the most of!

HOW TO FACE DYING IN A SPIRIT OF TRIUMPHANT OUTCOME

Since I maintain that the death-event can be a victorious experience, it is incumbent on me to suggest ways by which dying can be faced with a certain sense of dignity:

1. Don't Be Surprised By Death

I have two incidents in my files which clarify what I mean: Occasionally, while in a cemetery for a burial service, I will stroll around reading inscriptions on tombstones. A few years ago, I was in a country cemetery not far from Texarkana, Texas. I saw many tombstones with inscriptions, but the one that impressed me most stood erect where an older man had been buried. It read, "I expected this, but not just yet." Does not this reflect a common view toward dying—both our own and that of loved ones or close friends? Even for older persons? Pushed way back into consciousness is the inevitable, but it is never quite expected personally. The death-event is denied, ostracized, camouflaged, and spiritualized. The primary reason for this is fear. People are afraid of it because they don't understand it.

It was exactly 1:17 A.M. when the phone next to my pillow rang. The man on the other end of the line said, "Dave, it's Milly." "Milly" was the affectionate name given to Mildred, his devoted wife of many years. My friend burst into tears. I said, "Bob, tell me what's wrong." I didn't have the slightest idea, because six hours before his call we had laughed, joked, and thoroughly enjoyed each other's company at dinner. It had been only three hours since we said goodnight after a wonderful evening at the symphony. Voice quivering, Bob stumbled out the words, "Milly's dead." I could hardly believe it. She had been a genuine Christian, loving mother and grandmother, and a super church worker.

The words of Edmund Cooke are true:

> Death comes with a crawl,
> or comes a pounce,
> But whether he's slow or spry . . .
> You die." [3]

The element of surprise does not belong to the death-event. Defuse it by admitting that you will die. Is this to suggest that you should yearn for death? Of course, the answer is, "No." *Anyone who lives as fully as he should will not want to die.* He is filled with enough excitement about living that he feels like the retired school teacher who told me, "I want to hang around and see what happens next."

Rightly understood, dying respects and urges on life *now*. As Jesus said, "I am the resurrection and the life; he who believes in me, though he die, yet shall he live" (John 11:25, RSV). Pie in the sky in the sweet by and by is not the only pie for you to enjoy. The Psalmist spoke of the whole pie when he wrote, "For thou hast saved my life from death [this is the past], my feet from stumbling [this is the present], that I might live, ever mindful of God, in the sunshine of life [this is the future]" (Psalm 56:13, Moffatt).

2. Think of Dying As a Continuing Event in the Movement of Life

A loved one or close friend may die in an unnatural manner. He may have an early death. You and I may have an untimely death. In such cases, it is most difficult to think of death as a continuing event in the movement of life. This may also be true no matter when or how we die.

The main problem is our limited understanding of dying. As a result, we are prone to blot out of our minds any thoughts about dying, or we refuse to confront it, or we consider it a colossal catastrophe and double-decked disaster. With a condition like this, is it any wonder that everything connected with death leaves us cold and shuddering?

The new understanding needed is quite basic: *Physical death is as much a fact of life as birth!* Life consists of stages —birth, infancy, childhood, adolescence, adulthood, old age, and death. Jesus taught and showed the way to think of and experience death as a continuing event in the movement of life. "And taking the twelve, he said to them, 'Behold, we are going up to Jerusalem, and everything that is written of the Son of man . . . will be accomplished. . . . He will be . . . kill[ed] . . . *he will rise*'" (Luke 18:31–33, RSV, italics mine).

An unknown author spoke of it when he wrote:

> The tomb is not an endless night—
> It is a thoroughfare, a way

> That closes in a soft twilight
> And opens in eternal day.[4]

Aerzte'-Kalendar of Germany put it in reassuring terms. "The thought of death leaves me completely calm because I have the firm conviction that our spirit is a being of an indestructible nature, continuing from eternity to eternity; it is similar to the sun, which seems to set each night for us mortals, but which actually never sets, instead continues to shine uninterruptedly." [5]

The great truth is reflected by Paul when he wrote, "In *everything* [death, too!] God works for good with those who love him" (Rom. 8:28, RSV italics mine). As a continuing event in the movement of life, dying has the indelible impression of goodness upon it.

3. Accept Dying As a Dimension of Living

In her book, *On Death And Dying,* Dr. Elisabeth Kübler-Ross writes about five stages through which many dying people go—Denial, Anger, Bargaining, Depression, and Acceptance. At this point in my discussion, denial and acceptance are of interest.

When a person of any age is confronted with the news that he has a terminal illness, when he is made aware that no medical help holds the promise of restoring him to health, his first response is denial. "It isn't true." "You've made a mistake." "This cannot happen to *me.*" I was acquainted with an older person whose physician explained that medical science could do nothing about his disease. Angrily, he responded, "Nonsense! Besides I don't believe I have Hodgkins Disease." Elaborate tests had already confirmed his malady.

Dr. Ross describes this denial as a temporary defense. She tells of a middle-aged woman who had a visible, enlarged lacerative type of breast cancer, yet she refused treatment until a short time before she died. Her faith in her religion (one which tends to deny the reality of illness) was very strong, yet she finally submitted to hospitalization. Dr. Ross wrote, "As she grew weaker, her makeup became more grotesque. Originally rather discreetly applied red lipstick and rouge, the makeup became brighter and redder until she resembled a clown. Her clothing became equally brighter and more colorful as her end approached. During the last few days she avoided looking in a mirror, but continued to apply the masquerade in an attempt to cover up her increasing depression and her rapidly deteriorating looks." [6]

I believe that acceptance of death is the reply which denial needs. Don't confuse acceptance with an eager, happy, confrontation. Simply identify it with an admission of reality and positive adjustment to that reality. In this regard, acceptance depends on your concept of dying.

Do you view death as a disgrace and a disintegration of the person? The word Jesus used most often to describe his death is *glorify*. "The hour has come for the Son of man to be glorified" (John 12:23, RSV). The word used in the original language of the New Testament means honor, majesty, and splendid array. Then Jesus spoke of dying as a time of exaltation—not a tragedy, a perversion of justice, an accident, a colossal blunder in divine planning, and a withdrawal of God's love!

One of the outstanding surgeons specializing in the treatment of cancer said to me, "David, you'd be surprised the way many people, even professing Christians, act when they find out they're in the process of dying. They seem to feel God is hiding in the shadows somewhere, completely unrelated and unconcerned about their situation." The gap occurs when you fail to accept the humanity and divinity in the dying process.

In one sense, the reality of death carries a finality with it. The body is laid to earth. It returns ashes to ashes, dust to dust. But in a greater sense—the sense of the spirit, the basic person—dying is centrally a part of life and life is centrally a part of dying. Each person dies a little every day. Through this process, however, everyone picks up a little life every day; at least, this is the way it should be when dying is accepted as a dimension of life.

4. It's Okay to Feel The Agony of Dying

Sometimes, people try to buttress themselves against the inner pain which accompanies the process of dying. "I've got to act like a man," someone said. "I cannot let my feelings show . . . for the sake of my wife, children, and grandchildren." How unlike the example of Jesus!

"Now is my soul *troubled*," he said as the hour of death neared (John 12:27, RSV italics mine). "Disquieted" is the word used by Dr. James Moffatt; "My hour of heartbreak," according to Dr. J. B. Phillips; "My soul is in turmoil," is used in the New English Bible. On Golgotha's cross, Jesus cried, "My God, my God, why hast thou forsaken me?" (Matt. 27:46, RSV). Johann Heermann, the fifteenth-century hymnwriter, put the thought in these lines:

> For me, kind Jesus,
> was Thy incarnation,
> Thy mortal *sorrow,* and Thy
> life's oblation;
> Thy death of *anguish* and Thy
> *bitter passion*
> For my salvation.[7]

In the normal course of events, there is agony associated with dying; for instance, the temporary separation from loved ones and friends, the pain of termination from human relationships, the last cessation of earthly endeavors. There is a unique suffering to dying which no amount of stoicism can erase and no degree of Christian faith can eradicate. It is inhuman to act otherwise. Therefore, accepting death means accepting the suffering of dying.

To keep agony suppressed or repressed enlarges the suffering within you and prevents others from sharing it; they are not allowed the opportunity to help shoulder the load. You need their assistance, even if you do not admit it. And they need to help you so that they will more adequately bear the suffering of their own dying process when it comes.

You see, the suffering of dying and the new dimension of

life which dying ushers in points out the presence of sunshine and clouds simultaneously. Is not this a fact borne out over a lifetime—roses and thorns exist on the same bush? Try to deny the existence of the thorn and you find it pricks even harder. Acknowledge it, respect it, give it room, and you find greater ability to deal with the reality of it.

This agony can be subjugated through expression. Then it will be controlled!

5. It's Okay to Talk About Dying

The references to discussions by Jesus about his own death are numerous, particularly beginning with the eleventh chapter of the Gospel of John. But people now, especially Americans, treat the subject on a hush-hush level.

One of my older friends was dying as a result of collapsed lungs. The doctors knew it, his family knew it, I knew it, and he knew it. But would he talk about it? Never! During my last ten visits with him in the Intensive Care Unit, I posed the question in various forms, "Bob, you realize the seriousness of your condition. Do you want to discuss it?" He would not so much as acknowledge that the question was asked. Instead, he would tighten his lips, tense up, and grit his teeth.

Many people make every attempt to skirt the subject. They try to stay away from the elderly and terminally-ill persons. The excuse, "It's morbid, you know." Children are prevented from attending funerals or visiting relatives, even close relatives. The rationale is, "Oh, they're too young for that sort of thing." Or is the problem something deeper? Could it be that a shield is put between the living and the dying?

People act like dying doesn't exist. Talk about death with the dying is avoided. Family, friends, and even some doctors act as if the dying person doesn't have the right to know. Decisions are made for the dying when they are capable of making decisions for themselves or at least participating in the decision-making process. They could have input. Surely they deserve the dignity in their dying days which God has instilled in them as persons of worth.

After death, the body is beautified in an attempt to make it look like it did in life. People comment, "Oh, doesn't he look natural!" I have a growing dislike for our treatment of death and of those who are dying, because I see that these efforts constitute an incredible conspiracy of denial. They appear to be full of fakery, bordering on a farce, and, possibly, moral criminality. They demonstrate a loose and fragile idea of dying.

In my experience, *it has been proven that a person is better able to accept, understand, and cope with that which he knows*. A man with an incurable tumor of the brain stated, "I'm glad I know about it. I can handle it."

John was thirty-seven years of age, a brilliant industrial engineer, and a member of my church when he was told that he had leukemia. "Thank God, we talked about it," John said before he died. Rich was a successful, go-getter businessman when cancer was detected. The family told me that Rich didn't know about his condition. I was asked by the family not to leak the slightest word to Rich and I abode by their wishes until he, in desperation, said, "The doctors won't talk to me. My wife won't talk to me. The children won't talk to me. What's going on! And who do they think they're kidding!" He looked at me as he continued, "Mr. Ray, it would be easier if only someone would let me know. I need someone with whom to share my feeling." I became that someone.

Orville Kelly was told he had cancer and there was no hope for recovery. The whole family—Orville, wife, and teen-age children—struggled with this unexpected development. Out of it has come a wonderful organization called "Make Today Count" whose purpose is to help the terminally ill, their families and friends. As a guide, they use Orville's ten suggestions.

1. *Talk about the illness*. If it is cancer, call it cancer. You can't make life normal again by trying to hide what is wrong.
2. Accept death as a part of life. It is.
3. Consider each day as another day of life, a gift from God to be enjoyed as fully as possible.

4. Realize that life is never going to be perfect. It wasn't before and it won't be now.
5. Pray. It isn't a sign of weakness; it is your strength.
6. Learn to live with your illness instead of considering yourself dying from it. We are all dying in some manner.
7. Put your friends and relatives at ease. If you don't want pity, don't ask for it.
8. Make all practical arrangements for funerals, wills, etc. and make certain your family understands them.
9. Set new goals; realize your limitations. Sometimes the simple things of life become the most enjoyable.
10. *Discuss your problems with your family as they occur.* Include the children if possible. After all, your problem is not an individual one.[8]

Is all of this to say you should have your illness for breakfast, lunch, and supper? That you should make it the center of conversation and put it on a pedestal, like a little shrine, for all to see? No! I am advising, based on the example I see from Jesus as he approached dying, that you should be willing to talk about it.

6. Live Now in Such a Manner That Dying Doesn't Make You Ashamed

It was my privilege to get beyond the facade and down to the "guts" of life and death with a couple when the man's parents died in an automobile accident. They asked many questions about God, life, and death. I shared with them something that I have grown to believe and believe deeply; that is, *death is really a friend of life instead of its enemy.* Knowing that our years on earth are limited, we are encouraged to make life count.

A man of God underscored the brevity of life on this earth when he wrote, "A thousand years are but as yesterday to you! They are like a single hour! We glide along the tides of time as swiftly as a racing river, and vanish as quickly as a dream. We are like grass that is green in the morning but mowed down and withered before the evening shadows fall"

(Ps. 90:4–6, LB). A few verses later, he thought of the response adequate to brevity. "Teach us to number our days and recognize how few they are; help us to spend them as we should" (90:12, LB).

Rick Fox is one of the most touching examples of this that I know. He was a medical student in Houston. An honor student in high school, Rick was a top student in his class of young, aspiring doctors. He possessed such a love for medicine that he amazed the professors as well as fellow students. "Isn't it marvelous," Rick would often say, "we're going to be doctors and we've got to be good doctors."

In his second year at school, Rick became critically ill. In a few days, the doctor came into his hospital room, sat down on the edge of the bed, and said, "Son, I've got to tell you something. You have cancer." There was a silence.

Rick said, "Doc, is it terminal?"

"I'm afraid so."

"How long do I have?"

"Not long."

Then Rick said, "Let me have thirty minutes alone with God." The doctor quietly left the room. In thirty minutes, Rick called for him and the nurses. And he said, "I've settled it. I want to stay here in the hospital for you to use my body as a laboratory specimen. I'll keep a memo of my reactions so that my illness will help fight this terrible disease and cure others of it in the future."

Each day, the members of his class would come by and Rick would say to them, "We're going to be doctors and we've got to be good ones." He was told when he had only a few days left. He said that he wanted to go home and see his loved ones and the countryside. They put him in an ambulance and took the young man to the airport. There all sixty students in his class were lined up. In his wheelchair, he went down the line to say goodbye to each one. Before stepping inside the plane, he said, "We're going to be doctors. We've got to be good doctors." [9]

Tears flowed down all faces as that plane picked up speed, became airborne, and soon disappeared into the clouds. Ten days later Rick's body expired. I wonder what he talked over with God, other than what he could do to count for the rest of his days? I believe if we could have listened in, we would have heard, "Lord, I didn't ask for this. But I'm not afraid to die, because you've taught me how to live. I'll live that way as long as I'm here."

You may have passed Rick's age decades ago, yet your need is similar to his. Live in such a manner that dying doesn't make you ashamed. Are you fully alive? Are you optimistic and confident? Do you experience a joyous sense of well-being? Do you look forward to the day? Do you make plans believing you will succeed in them? Are you finding life interesting, exciting, and packed with possibilities of adventure? Do you expect good to come to you? Do you go forward to meet people eagerly, expecting to like them and them to like you? Is your chagrin over mistakes and failures transitory? *Are you God's person?*

7. Spend Extra Time Reading Your Bible

The Bible offers words of life by which to live and die. Those words are especially good for the dark hours. I have a friend who went through the most severe business reversal a person can imagine. He lost everything—position, power, prestige, and pay. A few days ago, I talked with him on the phone. He emphasized that he and his wife have dug into the Bible more than ever. Not given to any overly-emotional approach to religion, he claimed that, in a new way, they are discovering God working through the sacred pages, bringing growth and depth never before realized in their lives.

Given operating room, the Bible will help you discover possibilities in the crisis brought about by the dying process. It will show you that *a stumble may become a start, a need may become a nudge, an adversity may become an advance, and an end may become a beginning.*

The brilliant and very successful novelist, A. J. Cronin, is well known to readers. As a young man, he was a bright doctor in London's fashionable West End where he spent most of his time dithering over rich hypochondriacs. This didn't set well with him but he put up with it. Suddenly, the door to his career slammed shut. He became seriously ill with gastric ulcers and was told that he must take a long rest. The young man went to a bleak, rainswept, chilly little village in Scotland's highlands to spend six months. He was so depressed there that he almost despaired of life itself. He thought that all of his training had come to nought. "I'm at the end," he left. But he started hearing little dimly-perceived characters inside that cried out for release.

"Put us down on paper," they'd say. Cronin had never written anything in his life, yet he set his mind to it. About halfway through, he became so discouraged that he grabbed the manuscript and dumped it in a trash can. An old Scotsman persuaded him to retrieve it and continue. That book, his first, was the fascinating "Hatter's Castle," the beginning of a long string of bestsellers and the emergence of A. J. Cronin, one of the literary giants of modern times.

Yes, an end may become a beginning—when you honestly, openly, and seriously take the Bible as your chief resource book! Are you in need of hope? Read Psalm 18:28–29, 32 and Psalm 30:5. Do problems seem insurmountable? Read Psalm 25:15–18, and Psalm 34:18–19, and Philippians 4:13, 19. Are you upset? Read John 14:27 and Psalm 6:2–3. Is joy drained out of life? Read John 15:11 and 16:24. Would you like to have a fresh spurt of inner strength? Read Isaiah 40:28–31. They are words of comfort, understanding, peace, and love. The Bible gives you the long view and the upward view.

I emphasize *extra* time reading the Bible. Extra time includes empty times—times when you have nothing specific to do. A few minutes sitting, waiting, or at lunch. Take advantage of "little time" and you will grow into a much bigger person.

Even though you are an older person, you might find an updated translation more easy to read and understand; for example *The Living Bible, Paraphrased*, J. P. Phillips's translation, James Moffatt's translation, *The New English Bible*, the New American Standard Version, the Revised Standard Version, the *Good News Bible,* or *The Jerusalem Bible.* For poetic value, you may enjoy the King James Version.

Read some each day. Take your time because you have the time. Try to visualize what you read. Possibly some physical condition hampers your reading. Then ask someone to read to you. Of course, others will do it. I know an older person who is blind. Several young women in the neighborhood read to her and are glad to do it.

8. Face Dying With Confidence

In reference to his impending death, Jesus said, "The ruler of this world is coming. He has no power over me" (John 14:30, RSV). "I came from the Father and have come into the world; . . . I am leaving the world and going to the Father" (John 16:28, RSV). One of the questions put to me by an older person points out the gulf some people see between then and now. "Can such confidence be possessed by a human being in modern times?" One of the great purposes of Jesus was to show us what God is like and to convince us that we can and should have the qualities of God which we see in Christ. A person no different in capacity than you witnessed, "The Lord is my light and my salvation; whom shall I fear? The Lord is the strength of my life; of whom shall I be afraid" (Ps. 27:1, RSV).

The force which snips at confidence is the fear of dying. Yet, as Robert Burton stated, "Fear of death is worse than death." [10] Unmask the fear of dying and you will find it is a coward; it is no match for the tough realities of dying. It will lead a person to respond spinelessly to hard knocks, and it can easily scare him into defeat before the first punch is thrown.

Occasionally, boys have misunderstandings which they think will be solved through a fight. (That's nothing! Adults and nations do too, but their fights are glittered with intricate weapons and result in glamorized destruction!) A friend told me of one scrap he almost got into when he was ten years old. After the die was cast to have the fight, Harley wasn't sure he could win the match. The other fellow was bigger and older, so Harley, always a quick thinker, hurriedly changed his tactics. In effect, he began to snowball his freckle-faced opponent with scare talk. "You can't whip me, and you know it," he unflinchingly said. "Boy, if you tangle with me, I'm going to cream you and good." This verbal conditioning worked. Harley was amazingly convincing—to the point that he surprised himself. The other boy got scared, backed down, and was glad to squeak out of the tussle with only a skinned ego.

In a sense, the fear of dying hasn't a backbone that can stand up to the inner confidence which God is willing to share with you. The elimination, or, at least, minimization, of this fear of dying, can be experienced through a transforming act of God's love within you. There is the confidence factor.

9. Trust the Death-Event to God

Dying is an event common to all human life, but, as Alfred Lord Tennyson stated in his famous poem, *In Memoriam,* the commonness of death doesn't deaden or dull its keenness. He wrote:

> That loss is common would not make,
> My own less bitter, rather more.
> Too common! Never morning wore
> To evening, but some heart did break.[11]

The basic principle to which I direct your attention is this: *When god calls you (in life and in death, by whatever means), he calls you to a better, higher, and happier way than you knew before his call!*

Dr. Paul Tournier claimed, "All anxiety is reduced to anxiety about death. . . . Man carries death about within him all his life long, but it becomes more threatening as he grows old." I have been asked, "But do Christians accept death more readily than nonbelievers?" My reply: They *can,* but this does not mean all Christians do! Dr. Tournier wrote,

"We must admit that Christianity has done little to lessen the anxiety of the faithful in the face of death, despite its triumphant message about the resurrection of Jesus." [12] Is this the fault of people or the plan? I believe the error lies in understanding, acceptance, and trust.

The role of Christian faith is *not* to do away with dying on this earth. It is *not* to minimize death, much less eliminate it. The resurrection to life unending follows dying. Then the purpose of faith is to meet death and go through it. An unknown author expressed it in these lines.

> God's might to direct me,
> God's power to protect me,
> God's wisdom for learning,
> God's eye for discerning,
> God's ear for my hearing,
> God's word for my clearing.

The key word which applies is "trust." It isn't the load that weighs you down; it is the way the load is carried.

Jim Heneveld, a missionary in Mexico, told me that he learned to carry packs weighing over one hundred fifty pounds for many miles through the wilderness and jungle-like terrain characteristic of his area, and without getting tired, although he is a lanky one hundred seventy pounder. Jim said, "The people there taught me to put the weight at the right place. It will surprise you how much you can carry and where you can take it."

Dying is not too burdensome for you. Jesus said, "Come to me, all who labor and are heavy laden, and I will give you rest. . . . You will find rest for your souls. For my yoke is easy, and my burden is light" (Matt. 11:28–30, RSV). This is divine assurance that the burden is light enough for you to shoulder when the weight is put at the right place—in his hands!

M. Louise Haskins, in *The Gate of The Year*, gave insight to this matter. "And I said to the man who stood at the gate to the year: 'Give me a light that I may tread safely into the unknown.' And he replied, 'Go out into the darkness and put your hand into the Hand of God. That shall be to you better than light and safer than a known way.' " [13] As William Penn, one of the fathers of America, stated, "The end of life is to *know* the life that never ends." [14]

Scripture is resplendent with references to God's love for you, for example, "In all these things [trouble, pain, danger, threats, life, death, etc.] we are more than conquerors through him who loved us. . . . [nothing] will be able to separate us from the love of God in Christ Jesus our Lord" (Romans 8:37–39, RSV), Your response which brings the transforming, spiritual experience of this love to you is trust.

Some time ago, a thirty-mile stretch of an interstate highway in Louisiana hadn't been completed. The old two-lane highway motorists had to use had curves, and usually the traffic was heavy. It was particularly heavy one day as I traveled that road. Cars and trucks were almost bumper to bumper. I found myself behind a slow moving rig. Several times I edged toward the stripe in the middle of the highway, hoping I could pass him and get on to my engagement. However, I couldn't see in front of the truck, so I would pull back to safety. Eventually, the trucker realized my predicament. Soon, I saw a hand sticking out from the cab, motioning for me to pass, and I did.

Now, that hand could have been false. As far as I knew, it could have been wooden, a manikin. The trucker could have been playing a joke on me. I could have been tricked into thinking the way was clear when cars were speeding toward us. What made the difference? The reliability of the truck driver and my trust. I assumed he was real and the way was open for me to pass.

In essence, I trusted him. In this sense, I relied upon him, even to the tune of my life. Then, I acted upon trust by passing him. Spiritually, the act is similar to the case of the trucker and me. You depend on God, you rely on him, and you put the weight of your inner self into his hands. Your life, even in the process of dying, is entrusted to him. Writing from the crucible of such an experience, the Psalmist said, "Happy are those who are strong [trust] in the Lord, who want above all else to follow your steps. When they walk through the Valley of Weeping it will become a place of springs where pools of blessing and refreshment collect after rains! They will grow constantly in strength (Psalm 84:5–7, LB).

But how do you employ this spiritual trust? It *is* possible! It is surprisingly easy, if you want to have a spiritual relationship with God!

Several years ago, I put together a pamphlet entitled, "Discovery," in which I outlined the way to *experience* Christ within and to *live* each day, for as long as you possess life as a human, with Christ as your close companion. Possibly you will find it helpful.

The Need

Life

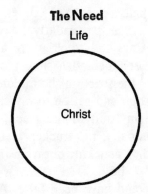

Christ

Self is the center of your life and keeps you from the vital relationship with God. Self is in charge. Self, by itself, is in the driver's seat.

The Answer

Life

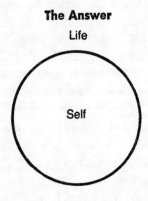

Self

Self needs to be replaced by Jesus Christ at the center of life. He is the link to God, and through him, God is brought into the center of your life. ". . . I myself [self alone] no longer live, but Christ lives in me" (Gal. 2:20, LB).

The Beginning

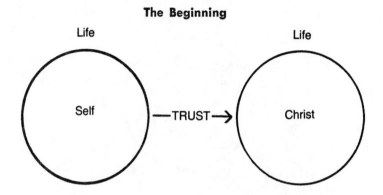

Life   Life

Self   —TRUST→   Christ

The way from self alone to Christ at the center of life is trust. This is faith exercised in your spiritual heart and demonstrated when you open yourself, as completely as you know and as much as you understand, to Christ. This is accomplished by prayer (conversation with God) in which you acknowledge that you are now trusting him.

It is a decision on your part: "Choose this day whom you will serve" (Joshua 24:15, RSV).

It is a definite, spiritual change: "When someone becomes a Christian he becomes a brand new person inside. . . . A new life has begun!" (2 Cor. 5:17, LB).

Like a gift, you receive him: "To all who received him, who believed his name, he gave the power to become children of God" (John 1:12, RSV).

Share the decision with someone as soon as possible. "Salvation that comes from trusting Christ . . . is already within easy reach of each of us; in fact, it is as near as our own hearts and mouths. For if you tell others with your own mouth that Jesus Christ is your Lord, and believe in your own heart that God has raised him from the dead, you will be saved. For it is by believing in his heart that a man becomes right with God;

and with his mouth he tells others of his faith, confirming his salvation" (Romans 10:8–10, LB).

You are now in partnership with God. You never need to be alone or have self at the center of life again.

The Result

Self is redeemed and revitalized by the love of Christ. Self is not X-ed out; your self is made new and enabled by God's power to develop positively. The response to God's love has given God the opening to claim you as a member of his spiritual family. You have allowed him to bring you inside the circle of forgiven people. Life is parlayed into victory. Dying is lifted to the point where it contains meaning.

The Continuation

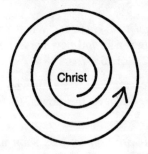

The beginning of your relationship with God on a personal basis was faith accepted. The continuation of the relationship is by *faith applied* through which this relationship expands. The Spirit of Christ enlarges throughout your life, like a ripple of water when a stone is tossed into the pond. The word is *grow*.

As long as you have capacity to think, *use the Bible each day*. It is the Discoverer's handbook; it is a road-guide for the Christian adventure.

Talk to God every day. This is prayer. Set aside private times in addition to sentence prayers throughout the day. Let God help you develop an attitude of prayer.

Share your Discovery with others and help them. Listen—Love —Lead—Share! You are now a channel instead of a reservoir.

Get active in a Church. Even if you are infirm, handicapped, and incapacitated, you can be active. Prayer for the church is activity and you can pray. The minister will gladly provide matters about which you can pray. Contact with the Church is activity and you can maintain contact with the Church. Sharing yourself through contributions is activity and you can give. Don't let the amount of the contribution keep you from this vital link to spiritual health. Any amount, given sincerely and according to your ability, is very important. Naturally, you can attend worship services, classes, and the organization for your age group as long as you are physically able.

Never wait for feeling. Act on the basis of faith—God's faith in you and your faith in him. Feeling will follow. After all, the act which has made you a member of God's family is not feeling, but your enlistment!

Consciously commit sins and problems to God as they come up. This keeps your relationship up to date.

Your life on this earth—remember, the death-event is an act of life—becomes a declaration of the relationship you have established with God. As Longfellow said, "And in the wreck of noble lives, something immortal still survives." [15]

> The Lord bless you and keep you;
> the Lord make His face shine upon
> you, and be gracious unto you.
> The Lord lift up His countenance

upon you and give you peace.
Now.
In the moment of dying.
Forevermore.
Amen.

Notes

A Word to the Reader

1. *The International Dictionary of Thoughts,* compiled by John P. Bradley, Leo F. Daniels, Thomas C. Jones (Chicago: J. G. Ferguson Pub. Co., 1969), p. 21.

2. Halford E. Luccock, *Never Forget to Live* (Nashville: Parthenon Press, 1961).

Chapter 1

1. "Living Productively to Be 100 Years Old," based on research by Robert Meyers, *Mainliner Magazine,* October 1972, pp. 32, 35.

2. Patricia McCormack, "Middle Age Begins at 25, AMA Says in New Study," *San Gabriel* [Calif.] *Valley Tribune,* 10 September 1972, p. 11-A.

3. Jan Barber, "Retiring Means Beginning Again," *Jackson* [Miss.] *Daily News,* 4 October 1974, p. 8-D.

4. Viktor Frankl, *Man's Search for Meaning* (New York: Washington Square Press, 1963), p. 179.

5. C. Duncan King, Jr., ed., *Journal of Religious Speaking,* November 1976, p. 42.

6. Ibid.

7. Ibid.

8. Osbert Sitwell, *The Man Who Lost Himself* (St. Clair Shores, MI: Scholarly Press, 1929).

9. George Gordon, Lord Byron, "On My Thirty-Sixth Year," *The Poems of Byron* (Boston: Houghton Mifflin Company, 1933), p. 206.

10. Robert Browning, "Rabbi Ben Ezra," *The Complete Poetical Works of Robert Browning* (Boston: Houghton Mifflin Company, 1895).

11. *Clergy Talk,* March 1976, p. 20.

12. "Fate slew him, but he didn't drop," *The Complete Poems of Emily Dickinson,* ed. Thomas H. Johnson (Boston: Little, Brown & Co., 1960), p. 60.

13. Frank C. Laubach, *Letters by a Modern Mystic* (New York: Student Volunteer Movement, 1937), p. 24.

14. George Shinn, *Good Morning, God* (New York: Hawthorn Books, 1976).

15. *International Dictionary of Thoughts,* p. 442.

Chapter 2

1. *Reader's Digest,* October 1976, p. 486.

2. Evelyn Underhill, *Mysticism* (New York: E. P. Dutton & Co., 1961).

3. Barber, "Retiring Means Beginning Again."

4. Joseph Lahey, "The Day I Stopped Feeling Ashamed," copyright *Guideposts Magazine,* appeared in *Jackson* [Miss.] *Daily News,* 7 April 1977, p. 10-A.

5. *Journal of Religious Speaking,* November 1976, p. 7.

6. "Emotions, Cancer Connection Found in Latest Studies," *Jackson* [Miss.] *Clarion-Ledger,* 7 June 1976, p. 18.

7. Ibid.

8. *Jackson* [Miss.] *Clarion-Ledger,* 4 March 1977, p. 15-A.

9. *International Dictionary of Thoughts,* p. 19.

10. Gerald Schomp, *Overcoming Anxiety* (Cincinnati: St. Anthony Messenger Press, 1976), pp. 103–105.

Chapter 3

1. Frank S. Mead, ed., *The Encyclopedia of Religious Quotations* (Old Tappan, NJ: Fleming H. Revell Co., 1965), p. 270.

2. *International Dictionary of Thoughts,* p. 23.

3. Ibid.

Chapter 4

1. *International Dictionary of Thoughts,* p. 19.

2. M. Shrout, M. Burnett, and M. Gifford, *Senior Adult*

Leadership Handbook (Jenkintown, PA: Louis Neibauer Co., Inc., 1976), p. 43.

3. *International Dictionary of Thoughts,* p. 24.

4. Louis Sabin, "4 Doctor-Athletes Prescribe Their Exercises for Health," *Parade Magazine,* 3 April 1977, p. 22.

5. Barber, "Retiring Means Beginning Again."

6. Walter E. O'Donnell, "How to Increase Your Energy," *Reader's Digest,* January 1977, p. 84. Originally appeared in *Woman's Day,* November 1976.

7. George Leonard, "Running for Your Life," *Reader's Digest,* January 1977, p. 50. Originally appeared in New West Magazine, 16 August 1976.

8. Ibid.

9. "How to Increase Your Energy," p. 84.

10. Jimmy Ward, "Covering the Crossroads," *Jackson* [Miss.] *Daily News,* 6 April 1977, p. 1-A.

11. Alfred Lord Tennyson, "Crossing the Bar," *Poetical Works of Tennyson* (Boston: Houghton Mifflin Company, 1974), p. 753.

12. "Coronaries Alien to Farm Life: Top Factor—Equanimity," *San Gabriel* [Calif.] *Valley Tribune,* 5 December 1971.

13. *International Dictionary of Thoughts,* p. 47.

14. Ibid.

Chapter 5

1. David Reuben, "How to Make the Magic Last," *Reader's Digest,* February 1976, p. 90.

2. Ibid., p. 91.

3. Ibid., p. 90.

4. Barber, "Retiring Means Beginning Again."

5. *Pomona* [Calif.] *Progress-Bulletin,* 14 August 1971, p. 9.

6. *Journal of Religious Speaking,* March 1977, p. 44.

7. Charles L. Allen, *Life More Abundant* (Old Tappan, NJ: Fleming H. Revell Co., 1968), p. 127.

8. *Journal of Religious Speaking,* April 1977, p. 17.

9. Ibid.

10. "Heroes and Hero-Worship: The Hero As a Priest," *Encyclopedia of Religious Quotations*, p. 306.
11. *Family Magazine*, 22 March 1970.
12. *Journal of Religious Speaking*, April 1977, p. 12.
13. J. A. Hadfield, *Psychology and Morals* (New York: Robert M. McBride & Co., 1928), p. 45.
14. Ovid, "Tristia," *Encyclopedia of Religious Quotations*, p. 271.

Chapter 6

1. Carl G. Jung, *The Undiscovered Self*, tr. R. F. C. Hull (Boston: Little, Brown & Co., 1958), p. 41.
2. Paul Tournier, *Learn to Grow Old* (New York: Harper & Row, 1972), p. 40.
3. Ibid.
4. Joyce Brothers, "Ask Dr. Brothers," *Jackson* [Miss.] *Clarion-Ledger*, 18 March 1977, p. 14-C.
5. Tournier, *Learn to Grow Old*, p. 2.
6. "End All Compulsory Retirement," *Dallas Morning News*, 17 July 1974, p. 7.
7. *International Dictionary of Thoughts*, p. 446.
8. "End All Compulsory Retirement," p. 7.
9. *International Dictionary of Thoughts*, p. 442.
10. *Journal of Religious Speaking*, January 1977, p. 5.

Chapter 7

1. *Journal of Religious Speaking*, February 1977, p. 24.
2. Ibid., p. 18.
3. Ibid., p. 22.
4. Napoleon Hill, *The Master Key to Riches* (Greenwich, CT: Fawcett Publications, 1965), p. 50.
5. Carl P. Rogers, "The Loneliness of Contemporary Man," *Journal of Religious Speaking*, January 1977, p. 53.
6. David Ray, *The Art of Christian Meditation* (Wheaton, Illinois: Tyndale House Publishers, 1977).
7. *The Presbyterian Outlook*, vol. 159, no. 18, 2 May 1977.

8. *International Dictionary of Thoughts,* p. 20.

9. Ibid., p. 445.

10. Ibid.

Chapter 8

1. "Are There Two of You?" *Civil Engineering,* October 1969.

2. Quoted in E. Stanley Jones, *How to Be a Transformed Person* (Nashville: Abingdon Press, 1951), p. 240.

3. *Journal of Religious Speaking,* March 1977, p. 52.

4. Teilhard de Chardin, *The Phenomenon of Man* (New York: Harper & Row, 1959), p. 283.

5. John E. Gibson, "How to Cope with Your Frustrations," *Family Weekly,* 1973.

6. *Journal of Religious Speaking,* December 1976, p. 37.

7. Don Muchmore, *The Los Angeles Times,* 30 September 1968.

8. "Letter to the Editor," *The Church Herald,* 29 April 1977, p. 21.

9. Lydell Sims, "Murphy's Laws Have Longer Arm," *Memphis* [Tenn.] *Press-Scimitar.*

10. *Clergy Talk,* January 1977, p. 16.

11. Ibid.

12. *International Dictionary of Thoughts,* p. 484.

13. Quoted in *The Christian Herald,* June 1977, p. 48.

Chapter 9

1. Dan Thrapp, "Easter's Story," *Los Angeles Times,* 2 April 1972, p. 12-A.

2. George Matheson, "O Love That Wilt Not Let Me Go," *The Hymnbook* (Philadelphia: The Publishing Agent), p. 400.

3. Edmund Vance Cook, "How Did You Die?" *Encyclopedia of Religious Quotations,* p. 100.

4. *Encyclopedia of Religious Quotations,* p. 97.

5. Ibid., p. 98.

6. Elizabeth Kübler-Ross, *On Death and Dying* (New

York: Macmillan Publishing Company, 1969), pp. 38–137.

7. "Ah, Holy Jesus, How Hast Thou Offended," *The Hymnbook*, p. 91.

8. "Orville Kelly's Ten Suggestions to Help Live with a Terminal Illness," *Guideposts Magazine*, April 1976, p. 5.

9. "The Rick Fox Story," Guideposts Magazine, February 1975, p. 26.

10. Robert Burton, "Anatomy of Melancholy," *Encyclopedia of Religious Quotations*, p. 99.

11. Alfred Lord Tennyson, *The Complete Poetical Works of Tennyson* (Boston: Houghton Mifflin Company, 1898), p. 164.

12. Tournier, *Learn to Grow Old*, p. 216.

13. M. Louise Haskins, *The Gate of the Year* (Toronto: Musson Book Company, 1940).

14. *Encyclopedia of Religious Quotations*, p. 272.

15. Henry Wadsworth Longfellow, "Building of the Ship," *The Poems of Longfellow* (Boston: Houghton Mifflin Company, 1922), p. 99.